Great Faithfulness

This is my story

Starla Joy Pöschl
Starla Joy Pöschl

Isaiah 25:1

GREAT FAITHFULNESS
©2012 Starla Joy Pöschl

All rights reserved. No part of this book may be reproduced in any form without permission in writing from the author, except in the case of brief quotations embodied in critical articles or reviews.

Scriptures taken from the Holy Bible, New International Version®, NIV®. Copyright © 1973, 1978, 1984, 2011 by Biblica, Inc.™ Used by permission of Zondervan. All rights reserved.

All hymn lyrics public domain, except "Great is Thy Faithfulness," ©1923, Renewed 1951, Hope Publishing Co, Used by permission.

Back cover photography by Carolin Schwaneberg.

Lulu Publishing
ISBN #: 978-1-105-14265-9

For Mom & Dad

Acknowledgements & Dedication

Without Jesus I wouldn't be who I am. In Him I live and move and breathe. Thank You, God, for life and for a love so great I can't begin to comprehend it. Your faithfulness is amazing. My life is Yours. I love You.

To my husband, Chris: thank you for cheering me on in this new venture. I couldn't have done it without your support and encouragement. Your love is beyond anything I dreamed was earthly possible, and I thank God for bringing me across the ocean to find you. I love you more than life.

My incredible children, David, Rebekah & Miriam, you are the best gift I could ever have received. I love being your mommy. I am so proud of each of you, and I love you through the whole universe and back — a zillion times!!!

Mom & Dad, where do I start? You have given me so much. Love, family, music, learning…the list goes on and on. But perhaps the two things that mean the most are the example of 61 years of a love-filled marriage and a heritage of those who love the Lord. You have been a blessing to countless many, and *I* am blessed beyond words to be your daughter. I love you more than words can say.

To my brother, Paul, and my sister, Victoria: thank you for loving me, despite my ruining everything by my arrival on the scene! You two have always been my heroes. I love you. (And, no, you don't get 95% as my managers!) Lehann & Charlie, you have made our family beautifully complete.

To Mum & Dad (a.k.a. Angela & Wolfgang Poeschl), Phil & Karina, and Nick: thank you for so readily and lovingly taking me in as daughter & sister. I will never cease to be grateful for having been twice blessed when it comes to family. All my love.

Steven, Andrea, Caleb, Chris, Nathaniel, Jeff, Erin, Lisa, Lukas & Dominik: you all make me proud to carry the title Aunt! Each of you has expanded what I call family, and I love you for it. May you each see the love and faithfulness of God in your life.

To Julie Weston, my own Diana: thank you for encouraging this Anne to write. There has never been a more bosom friend. Alatsamse.

A very big thank you to my friend, Stephani McGirr, for your invaluable help (in the midst of life with four children!) with editing, but even more for your friendship in this beautiful country to which God has brought us.

Special thanks must finally go to Linda Crawford. Without you I'd probably still be thinking about finishing this book! Thank you for encouraging my writing and for believing in me. You have no idea how much that means to me. Much love comes from Austria to you.

Great Faithfulness

Acknowledgements & Dedication 5

Introduction 9

Exposition 11

1 **Blessed Assurance**. 15
   This is my story

2 **Stand Up for Jesus** 23
   When I just want to sit

3 **Where He Leads I'll Follow** 31
   Even across the pond

4 **Saviour, Like a Shepherd Lead Us**. 37
   A companion for the journey

5 **I Need Thee Every Hour**. 44
   Especially at 4:30 a.m.

6 **Just As I Am** 53
   With ketchup in my eyes

7   **Sweet Hour of Prayer** 61
Or at least 2 minutes

8   **Faith Is the Victory** 67
Overcoming my JFK world

9   **'Tis So Sweet to Trust in Jesus** 75
Simple – just not so easy

10   **Oh, to Be Like Thee** 81
I'll let Rebekah do it

11   **The Solid Rock** 87
My hope – and house – are built on nothing less

12   **How Firm a Foundation** 93
It's the bricks that are sometimes a bit wobbly

13   **Jesus Will Walk with Me** .99
In joy and in sorrow

14   **Day By Day** 107
Riding life's roller coaster

15   **He Keeps Me Singing** 113
Fills my every longing

16   **Great is Thy Faithfulness** 117
All I have needed

Recapitulation 121

Introduction

As I have considered the writing of this book, my past has come to memory in full force. Though a glance through the chapter titles may suggest otherwise, this is not a book about hymns. However, those old songs of the church have been such an enormous influence in my life that as I thought about how I wanted to go about putting things together, hymn titles—not chapter titles—kept coming to mind. This is not really that surprising. Growing up in a pastor's home, surrounded by music, hymns were as much a part of my diet as mom's pancakes and brownies.

Pictures come to mind of myself as a 6-year-old, in the church orchestra with my violin, sitting next to my mom on one of those small green Sunday School chairs so my legs could reach the floor. My fingers followed hers on the violin, not yet being able to read the notes in the hymnbook. My sister, Victoria, sat a couple rows behind me with her saxophone—my brother, Paul, at the back with his baritone piping out the bass line to "Camping in Canaan." Mrs. Johnson was on my other side with her violin, and Dayna was at the back playing her sax while changing the overheads for the choruses that we did sing—after the hymns, of course. Her father, Bill Evans, head usher and altogether wonderful, stood at the back of the church conducting us all over the heads of the congregation. Miss Stewart was at the piano playing the introductions for us in all her classical glory. When Dad wasn't playing along on his mandolin from the platform, he was leading the congregation from the pulpit, booming out, "In----my----heart----there----rings a melody...."

Hymns seemed to be everywhere for me. The standards in *Little House on the Prairie*, my favorite TV show (and one of the only I was allowed to watch), were "Ring the Bells of Heaven" and "Bringing in the Sheaves," which I never did get. Nor did Michelle Johnson ever get over "*Beulah Land?!*" My mom had her hilarious piano renditions of "When the Role is Called Up Yonder" and "Leaning on the Everlasting Arms," which to her feigned dismay are still requested on occasion. I can tell you even now that #200 in our church's old hymnbook was "Nothing but the Blood," and #1 in the new book was "O Worship the King". Margaret Jensen's stories were accompanied by "'Tis So Sweet to Trust in Jesus", making Mama's kitchen come alive to all of us. "He the Pearly Gates Will Open" was sung in Norwegian at so many Scandinavian events that I could sing it before I even understood what I was singing!

All that to say, please indulge me as I bring you my story, accompanied by songs learned in infancy, coming back again and again over the years. Some of the verses are included, and I know they will bless the reader. They may not have much to do with anything in this collection of stories, but they might have triggered the memories that have shaped the writing. For me these songs are a part of an incredible heritage which has shaped in many ways who I am. For some they may be familiar, for others utterly unknown. But here they are. May they stand as declarations of the truths of the Word of God. Great is His faithfulness.

Exposition

    The sun is beginning to set, and I'm sitting here at my desk overlooking the city. The shadows are getting very long, and soon the last rays of the day will sink behind the nearby hills. The mist has set in, giving off a blue haze and sending out the call for evening. A golden dome in the distance reflects the fading light, piercing the panorama like a lone star. In the foreground is a band of trees, not yet in their fall glory, but dressed in every shade of green imaginable, stretched out like a prelude to one of the most beautiful cities of the world. Vienna. The city of music. The heart of Europe. The strolling grounds of the greatest composers the world has ever known. And from my own window, I can watch as it lights up, getting itself ready for concert-goers and opera lovers to enjoy the wonders of music.

    As I contemplate the great faithfulness of God, I am in awe of His ways. They are definitely not my ways! My plans over the years have come and gone, but God truly has directed my life. How is it that I sit here, reveling in His goodness to me? How is it that I sit here, enjoying His blessing in these incredible surroundings? And even more, how is it that I sit here, daring to put into words on paper the great faithfulness of God in my life? Though I did find my first gray hair at age 30, I am after all only 33, and I know that I have many more years of experiencing that faithfulness. I have not yet celebrated my 10th wedding anniversary, and I know that I have much more to learn when it comes to marriage. My children are only 3 and 5, and I know that I have many more years of parenting lessons ahead. But nonetheless, here I sit, compelled to share the faithful God stories that I have collected thus far, though I may be not even halfway through my journey. May these pages be an encouragement to hold on, and may they serve as yet another reminder of God's great faithfulness.

Brunn am Gebirge, Austria
September, 2006

13

Blessed Assurance

Frances J. Crosby, 1873

Blessed Assurance, Jesus is mine!
Oh, what a foretaste of glory divine!
Heir of salvation, purchase of God,
Born of His Spirit, washed in His blood!

This is my story, this is my song,
Praising my Saviour all the day long.
This is my story, this is my song,
Praising my Saviour all the day long.

Perfect submission, perfect delight!
Visions of rapture now burst on my sight!
Angels descending, bring from above
Echoes of mercy, whispers of love.

Perfect submission, all is at rest.
I in my Saviour am happy and blest;
Watching and waiting, looking above,
Filled with His goodness, lost in His love.

You have given me the heritage of those who fear Your name.
Psalm 61:5

1
Blessed Assurance
This is my story

My story starts in 1950, when Ruth Eide married Eldred Nelson, forming the beginning of what would be my family. My mother grew up in Anaconda, Montana, and my dad was raised in various places in Michigan. That one chapter of *their* story would end up in Austria is one of God's mysterious ways.

My mother, born in 1928, came from a Christian, Scandinavian home. Her father was the stricter side of the parental unit. He didn't often see the humorous side of things, which caused him considerable distress when Uncle Charlie, my mom's brother, came along. In Grandpa's house, you didn't get sick on a school day, and also never on Sunday, which only left Saturday, which was the only day any child in the house ever got sick. This is what I was told, though my memory is of him always singing something, with the cupboard always producing a cookie when I came to visit. Grandma, on the other hand, was known always to have a twinkle in her eye, pulling practical jokes on my mom and her three brothers. My own brother and sister remember this side of Grandma, but I was 3 three months old when she died.

However, her humor was passed down through her children, and more than once my ice cream disappeared when I wasn't looking, although Mom's red face and silent laughter were usually a pretty good indication that I'd find it in her possession under the table. This strain of fun has served me well, as I seemed to have married into a European counterpart, where I have had to learn to give as good as I get!

My father, born in 1927, became a Christian at 14, shortly after his brother, after which the whole family came to know faith. Dad has told us many stories about his childhood, which was anything but wealthy. "I wasn't born with a silver spoon in my mouth." We heard about the snow blowing in between the logs of the cabin at Lost Lake, coming to rest on the blankets as they slept. We heard about Grandma's amazing ability to cook incredible food from nothing (the incredible part we experienced ourselves years later!). We heard about walking in the snow 8 miles to school, barefoot, uphill both ways (he denies that one now!). We heard about how "in my day, we wore jeans because we were poor!" We heard about how his dad yodeled all the time, a talent which was apparently hereditary, since our own house was always filled with yodeling. Dad's even famous for his yodeling now. I figure that must be why I ended up so near the Alps!

Mom and Dad met at Central Bible Institute in Missouri, and dad followed mom back to Montana, married her and had a 6-day honeymoon as they drove to their first pastorate in the panhandle of Idaho. At 23 and 22, Dad pastored the little church, mom played the piano, and they loved and lived there for 6 years, getting firewood as gifts, chopping heads off chickens (loving thy neighbor in ways we would never dream!), and hoping enough money would come in the offering plate to make it through the week. Spokane, Washington, was the next stop where 12 years of their life were spent. Here, after being married for 13 years having had no children, they decided to adopt. Paul was 11 weeks old when he arrived, and 2 years later 3-week-old Victoria came to complete the family. God had blessed them tremendously, and life was good. (And Paul and Victoria, you don't need to add that it should've stayed that way!)

Mom and Dad then felt God was calling them to move to western Washington to pastor Des Moines Assembly of God, just south of Seattle. They settled down and proceeded to carry out God's work. Then they had a big surprise. My brother and sister to this day persist in calling it an accident. In any case, 23 years after they were married, when Mom was 45 and Dad 46, I was born to them. They were called Abraham and Sarah (this was 1973 — when it wasn't as common as it is now to have a baby when you were over 40). Paul and Victoria, then 10 and 8, had a baby sister, and they did love me, no matter what they say! And so we became 5.

I grew up much-loved and loving much. Victoria was my big sister who could do no wrong. She also prepared me for future hairdressers with her no-mercy hairbrush. Paul was my role model — whatever he liked I did, too, and vice versa. Thanks to him I didn't know that I liked any other fish than tuna in a can until I was 12.

They also discovered that they had a willing slave, getting them whatever they wanted, at least until I was old enough to realize I had the right to protest. But they were good to me, even taking me along to the pizza parlor with their youth group friends. I never did ask if Mom made them do that. But I'm sure she didn't — they loved me! And I'm sure I never got on their nerves. Ah, well — ignorance is bliss, they say.

Only much later in life did I realize that they weren't altogether perfect (sorry, in a book the truth must come out). They do still say, however, that through adoption they are the "chosen ones", and I am the other "issue" of Mom and Dad's marriage, as was stated on their will for years after my birth. I was certainly glad when that detail was taken care of, I must say. Family life was good — great, as far as I was concerned.

We experienced a lot as a family whose life centered around the church. The good, the bad and, yes, even the ugly. People came and went. Some stayed. But in everything, God was faithful. And there was always enough. I wore hand-me-downs a lot, which I thought was great — not only was the dress beautiful, but it used to be so-and-so's! My daughter, Rebekah, feels the same way now. (Although the other day she did get very excited to have shiny new dress shoes — "that no one has ever worn before!")

Anyway, as far as I was concerned, we were rich. The smell coming through the door after Sunday School and morning service proved it. Mom's roast had cooked to perfection while we were gone, and Dad couldn't get the potatoes mashed fast enough — although that had to wait until after he changed out of his suit and tie.

I never knew Sunday to be a day of rest — not in our house, anyway. After lunch and Dad's nap, it was back for evening service, where I would fall asleep on the front pew (only when I was little, believe me!). Dad didn't forbid us to get sick on a Sunday like Grandpa, but I do remember being somewhat miserable and lying on the couch in Dad's office, waiting for service to end.

Sunday meant church. That was normal life in our home, and no one ever questioned it. I never could understand those people who didn't come on a Sunday evening. Or who went camping over a weekend and missed church. Unheard of. And to this day I am one of the few who almost always wears a dress to church — somehow it's ingrained in me as the 11th commandment. When I was last in Seattle, Mom wore trousers to church — probably for the first time in 79 years. I thought the world was coming to an end.

All that to say, God was always the central figure in my life. Jesus was the friend who was always there – "the head of this house, the unseen guest at every meal, the silent listener to every conversation" – from the plaque hanging close to the kitchen table. Far from threatening, that was a good thing. Dad's prayers after breakfast were as expected as the Grandma's Molasses mom spooned down our throats before we left for school each morning – only much more welcome.

As long as I can remember God was with me and I loved Him. I don't know when exactly I "got saved." I used to hate when people would ask me that, because I couldn't give them some date, made holy by my decision. That used to bother me, until many years later I heard J. John (an English evangelist) say that if you don't know the day you became a Christian, "look around to see if there's evidence that you were born." It reminds me of my children's video where Tigger doesn't know when his birthday is, and he starts to worry that he was never born. I don't need a date to be able to know that Jesus made a difference in my life.

We also had a small Christian school connected to the church – the result of my dad's vision and prayer. What a different way to grow up. I was the top of my graduating class – all 4 of us! I grew up with the Bible surrounding me on all sides. I took it for granted then, but it is such a part of me now. I'm so thankful for that heritage.

To balance things out, I participated in the youth orchestra in Seattle, having started violin lessons at age 3 (Mom thought she'd get me a toy violin, then she found out how much they cost – it was no longer a toy!). Music was everywhere in my life, and extremely important to me. So much so that I never even went skiing for fear of breaking an arm or finger and not being able to play. Some of the best skiing ever was 45 minutes from home, yet I never had a ski on my foot until I was in Switzerland at age 23. And there it was cross-country skiing — that, of course, could do no harm and is so much easier. HA!

Yes, well, back to the music. I took violin lessons until I graduated from high school, somewhere in there knowing that this was what God meant for me to do always. Mrs. Weiss started me when I was little, wearing white tights to every lesson, and continued on (as Mrs. Nicks after her marriage) even when all Mom did was drive me to the lesson and then fall asleep (and snore) at the other end of the room.

Youth Symphony introduced me to a whole new world of music and friends, and proved again that God is faithful everywhere. Prayer took on a whole new meaning on audition days. "Please let me not be so nervous that my bow just bounces down the strings and I make a total fool of myself." Those years were wonderful — and full of a lot of practicing. I also took piano lessons with Mrs. Hall. She taught me so much more than the notes. Her love of music was contagious. Violin remained my main focus, however, and as I got older, Mrs. Nicks challenged me to do more, and I took the challenge and loved it. I played all over, both in churches, with Mom on the piano, and in classical concerts and competitions. After a neighbor paid me $60 to play background music while he proposed to his girlfriend on the ferry, Paul and Victoria offered to be my managers at a mere 95% commission. Aunt Karen's offer of 75% was better, but I managed myself somehow, with Mom's help, and that was free.

When I think of my spiritual journey until I went to college, there are too many memories to record — some in pictures that flash across the screen of my growing-up years. Mrs. Bates praying for me as a young girl at the altar at the end of a Sunday evening service. Dad preaching on choices and habits in Wednesday school chapel. The children's crusade where the black light brought to life the reality of the nails in Jesus' hand when He died for *me*. Evangelist Joe Pyott's challenging sermons. Missionary speakers with their slide shows, giving me an awareness of the bigness of the world and the universal need for Jesus. Youth group meetings when it was much more than just fun. Missionette evenings where Bible reading became more than just the means of getting more Skittles from Mrs. Wood. Books read for school written by men and women who gave their very lives for the love of the ones Christ loved. Mom's reminder through my tears that bitterness against those who hurt us only does damage to ourselves. Testimonies of people in the church who were sustained or transformed by the Holy Spirit's power. On and on it could go. Some of those times became even more relevant in later years.

There are so many instances, looking back, where I see God at work in my life, quietly shaping and directing me, letting me grow through the good and the not-so-easy. Again, it would take too many pages to record them all. This little glimpse is just a few measures in the first movement of the symphony God is writing. It is as yet unfinished. But there is a refrain that keeps repeating again and again — the theme: God is faithful. He was always there. When friends abused trust and disappointed. When church seemed to be more about hurting than helping. When things went a bit differently than you had planned. But in everything, there was the knowledge that I was never alone. The knowledge that "in all things God works for the good of those who love Him, who are called according to His purpose." (Romans 8:28) What a promise. What comfort. And what a heritage to have received. To know without a doubt, even if you don't always understand it, that God is faithful.

What blessed assurance. Jesus is mine. This is my story.

Stand Up for Jesus

George Duffield Jr., 1858

Stand up, stand up for Jesus,
Ye soldiers of the Cross.
Lift high His royal banner;
It must not suffer loss.
From vict'ry unto vict'ry,
His army shall He lead,
Till ev'ry foe is vanquished
And Christ is Lord indeed.

Stand up, stand up for Jesus.
The trumpet call obey;
Forth to the mighty conflict,
In this His glorious day.
"Ye that are men now serve Him,"
Against unnumbered foes;
Let courage rise with danger,
And strength to strength oppose.

Stand up, stand up for Jesus —
Stand in His strength alone.
The arm of flesh will fail you —
Ye dare not trust your own.
Put on the gospel armor
And, watching unto prayer,
Where duty calls or danger,
Be never wanting there.

You will be my witnesses in Jerusalem, in all Judea and Samaria, and to the ends of the earth.

Acts 1:8

2
Stand Up for Jesus
When I just want to sit

    The plane rose higher and higher in its ascent from SeaTac airport. My heart rate responded to the significance of the accumulating distance. The day had come. I had said my goodbyes and now was on a flight bound for Boston—alone. Several months before I had made the trip to Boston with my mom to audition at New England Conservatory of Music, where I wanted to study violin with James Buswell. I had met Mr. Buswell when I played in a master class at age 16, and through further contact that year, it was clear that I would study with him in Boston. At 17 I finished high school, and graduation was a celebration of that first major milestone. At the same time I looked forward to the next stage of the journey. I was ready to take what I had learned from Mrs. Nicks, Mrs. Hall and the years I spent in the youth symphony and embark on a new musical adventure.

    The February trip to Boston with mom had been wonderful. We stayed with friends there and saw the sights. The city was incredible. My audition came and went, with plenty of nervous moments in between. But all the preparation paid off, and a month later I received the letter of acceptance. August was spent packing and repacking, trying to decide how much of my life would fit into two suitcases. Excitement is hardly expressive enough for my state of mind.

The events leading up to that solo cross-country flight had been so obviously orchestrated by God that I didn't doubt for a moment His leading. I had seen His faithfulness again and again. However, sitting on that plane, alone with my thoughts, excitement slowly began to swing like a pendulum over toward anxiety. The future loomed before me, totally unknown. My anxiety heightened as the plane rose. We flew into the low cloud cover not uncommon in Seattle, and my emotions hovered between the two extremes. As we rose higher still, the clouds began to thin, and suddenly the sun broke through. The plane turned towards the east, and I looked out the window to the south. There, large as life, was Mount Rainier, rising far above the clouds, in all its beauty and glory.

Suddenly I knew the message was for me. God was still there. Faithful. Even more so than my mountain which had been there, steady and unchanging, as long as I could remember. Above the clouds of my fears and uncertainties, God was there, steady and unchanging. That wouldn't change, just because I left one coast to go to the other. I hung on to that promise. As we flew over the Cascade Mountains, God's peace replaced the anxiety that had threatened to overwhelm me. I would make it. To this day, seeing Mount Rainier from the plane is as sure a declaration of God's presence and faithfulness as if He were to speak the words aloud.

Leaving Seattle and moving to the other side of the world—okay, country, although it felt like the ends of the earth—was an enormous step. Now I know it was just a preparation for later. Moving from Seattle and all that it represented to Vienna directly would have been unheard-of. But I had no idea of that at the time.

I was away from home for the first time. Away from not only family and friends, but also away from the sheltered environment in which I had existed. I think I had no idea what was really coming. It wasn't just the noise of the big city — at all hours of the day and night — or the intensity of the music world behind the practice room door. NEC (New England Conservatory) was anything but Christian. I had been in a school where there was a 6-inch rule between girls and boys (no kidding!). The closest thing to that now was that guys weren't allowed in the bathroom on our floor of the dorm. Though I did encounter a guy there once, and it wasn't the plumber, hugging the commode, drunk and miserable.

What a shock. The whole thing. But one of my first memories of that first week — during orientation — was walking through the halls, and right next to the Beethoven statue was a table with some Christian books, pamphlets and Gideon Bibles. I stopped to have a look. The man there was Scott Cowan, a jazz professor and leader of the Christian Fellowship at NEC.

That group turned out to be my lifeline. I found others whose faith was more important than spending that extra hour and a half on Friday afternoon in the practice room. It was there that I was encouraged to hang on and live out the gospel in the midst of an unbelieving world. It was there that I took the risk of leading a women's Bible study, where friends became sisters in that place far from home. It was there that I discovered the absolute necessity of Christian fellowship to keep one's eyes on the right path. It was there I learned that God was wherever I was, even in the "secular" school where I had chosen to earn my degree. "Secular" means without God, and God was with me there, so it was no longer "secular" — it became a sacred place where He taught me more than I could ever have imagined.

It was during these years that I learned to really make my faith my own. One valley-to-mountain-top experience happened early into my freshman year. Freshman Seminar was a required liberal arts class, in which all kinds of things were explored, to expand our minds, I guess. The professor was fantastic, and I enjoyed the class until we had to read a book by Freud. Our assignment at the end of the book was to take a chapter—assigned, not chosen—and make a presentation. I was given, of course, the only chapter in which he quoted Scripture. I should say misquoted Scripture.

I took it as both a challenge and an opportunity to stand up for God's Word. In essence I illuminated the misquotation, which then unraveled his whole argument in the entire chapter. I sat down, feeling pretty good about it, until Mr. Klein got up to comment on it after. He proceeded, as an educator, to play devil's advocate to everything I had said. It wasn't to tear my presentation apart, but really to stretch me and my observations. I understood on an intellectual level what he was doing, but emotionally I was devastated. I went back to my room, curled up on my bed and cried.

An hour later I had a lesson scheduled, and I decided to go even though I was a wreck. The weekly lesson was the main reason for being there, so I went. Before I went to NEC, we had known of the strong Christian heritage of my teacher, Mr. Buswell, but since I had been there, it had not really come up that much in my interaction with him on a musical level.

When I arrived that day for my lesson, it was evident that I had been crying (to this day if I cry one tear it is obvious to all for the whole of the next day!). Not going into details, I said that I would make it through the lesson and so we went ahead. I recorded the rest of the experience in my journal at the time:

"13 December 1991

"He finished [the lesson] a bit early...and asked me what was wrong. I started to explain—with quavering voice. When I go to the Freud part, he totally understood and gave me a hug. I lost it. The stress just seemed to have built up and needed release.... He had me sit down on the couch and just talked to me for a long time. He was just like a father. It was as if daddy couldn't be there, so he stepped in. It was wonderful. But the crowning glory came right at the end. We were sitting there—me sniffing away and trying to wipe away my tears—when suddenly he started to pray. He prayed for me! It was wonderful. I had never heard him pray before, and here he was praying with and for *me*! It was so beautiful. It could have been dad. I left there with such gratitude welling up inside of me. Here I am, at a secular school, with a violin teacher who can pray with me! God is so good. He knew that I needed that right then. I left that room, and I knew that everything was going to be okay. And with God's help, it was."

That moment was for me one of the biggest demonstrations of the faithfulness of God, no matter where we are. Though it may seem insignificant in the greater scheme of things, it was a turning point for me in my faith. I had stood up for Christ, then felt like I had been completely trampled over, and yet God with such great love showed me He cared, and even that He was pleased, even though it didn't produce the results *I* was looking for. He was faithful.

There were so many times where I can look back and see God's hand at work through those four years in Boston. He provided me with family—Aunt Jan and Uncle Jud Carlberg, president of Gordon College, just outside the city. They are cherished family friends, and they took me in as a niece. I spent many holidays and weekends with them—soaking in their love and wisdom—learning life and love for God. I also had a church family at North Shore Assembly of God. Every Sunday Maurine and her girls picked me up from the T (subway) and drove me to church. And most of the time I went home with Sam and Bridget to enjoy Sunday lunch with them and Sam's (cute and single!) brothers. God was with me. There was no doubt about it.

The other milestone in my spiritual journey at this time came in my junior year. In our Christian Fellowship, I had learned to love people from many different denominations, finding the common denominator in a relationship with Jesus, despite differing doctrinal issues. It was in a conversation with a Christian friend when God taught me something huge, though I didn't realize it until much later.

We were walking along the big fountain by the Christian Science church around the corner from NEC, and he was debating with me the gifts of the Holy Spirit, which in his view were only for New Testament times. I strongly disagreed, yet for every point I brought up, he had a very convincing argument. Getting more and more frustrated, I eventually ended up in tears (yes, they come aggravatingly easily!).

Finally, I stopped, wanting to just sit down and end the miserable exchange. I said I didn't have any more answers, except to say that I had experienced the power of the Holy Spirit, and I knew it was real. I was completely defeated and devastated at my inability to stand up for what I believed. It wasn't until sometime after that conversation, which played horribly over and over again in my mind, that I realized the truth in my final declaration.

I may not ever be able to convince anyone of anything on an intellectual level, but no one can ever take away my own experience. That is my most powerful testimony. I know that God is real, that Jesus is the friend who never fails, and that the Holy Spirit lives in me and that His joy is my strength (Nehemiah 8:10). I have experienced it over and over in my life, and no one can convince me otherwise.

I look back at that conversation, at the prayer encounter with my violin professor, at the people God had lined up along the way, at the conferences and retreats which fed my soul in a dry and thirsty land, and I see again the faithfulness of God in every step. That alone is enough to make me continue to stand up for Jesus, even when I just want to sit. And I've also learned, even when I do sometimes sit, I find Him sitting there next to me, waiting for me to find the strength — His joy, my strength — to get up and go on, with Him. He is faithful.

Even if Mount Rainier does blow its top one day in the predicted volcano, He'll still be there!

Where He Leads I'll Follow

Ernest W. Blandly, 1890

Sweet are the promises; kind is the Word
Dearer far than any message man ever heard
Pure was the mind of Christ, sinless, I see
He the great Example is, and Pattern for me

Where He leads I'll follow, follow all the way
Where He leads I'll follow, follow Jesus ev'ry day

Sweet is the tender love Jesus hath shown
Sweeter far than any love that mortals have known
Kind to the erring one, faithful is He
He the great Example is, and Pattern for me

List to His loving words, "Come unto Me!"
Weary, heavy-laden, there is sweet rest for thee
Trust in His promises, faithful and sure
Lean upon the Saviour, and thy soul is secure

Then Moses said to him, "If your Presence does not go with us, do not send us up from here."

Exodus 33:15

3
Where He Leads I'll Follow
Even across the pond

Books lined the polished wood shelves on every wall of the room. Rich red-toned oriental carpets and brass lamps giving off a soft light completed the effect. It was everything you would expect from an intimate library at Harvard. I was there to meet the woman with whom I wanted to study in Germany. I was in the process of applying for the Beebe Grant for Musicians. Coming to this private chamber music concert was another step towards my goal: a year of study abroad. This grant was based in Boston, and with much pleasure I had come back to the east coast to audition for the grant, meet my would-be professor and conveniently to visit friends. After the concert, I played an informal audition, and was given an encouraging verbal acceptance that if I received the grant, she would teach me. It was a bit of a surreal experience, but I left confident that God was truly guiding my steps.

I had received my Bachelor of Music degree just under a year before and had gone back to Seattle to become a student no longer, but rather a contributing member of society—to teach violin, get my Suzuki teaching certificate and work as a free-lance musician. Graduation from NEC had been wonderful. Our own Jordan Hall was being restored at the time, so we had to "settle" for having our ceremonies down the street at Symphony Hall. A few days before I had had the unforgettable experience of playing in our commencement concert in Symphony Hall, conducted by Seiji Ozawa. It was a fantastic finale to my four-year sojourn in Boston. I had grown up during those years in Boston. God had revealed Himself to me in so many ways, and I learned much which unknowingly prepared me for what He had in store.

Back in Seattle there was one more dream still waiting to be fulfilled. My European experience. Ever since I was eleven years old and with my parents visited relatives in Scandinavia, the desire to return had been increasing. With that goal in mind I had applied for scholarships and made audition tapes. Thus I found myself back in Boston for the Beebe Grant audition and subsequently in the Harvard library, watching like an observer as my future unfolded incredibly before me.

My audition for the grant went really well, and not long after arriving back in Seattle I received the letter telling me I had won the audition and the money was mine for study in Germany. Wow. Home of Bach, Beethoven and Brahms. I was ecstatic! I had taken a year of German at the community college near our home, and now I would be able to use it! I wrote to the professor in Germany to inform her of my news and to inquire how I should go about things with her there at the university where she taught. Her reply was not exactly what I expected. Looking back, it is so clear to me that God's hand was directing my course, although I thought everything was falling apart. She informed me, in a nutshell, that it was not going to work out to study with her, because of difficulties with university policies, blah, blah, blah. Whatever the reasons were, which I didn't really understand, they completely messed up my plans. What was I supposed to do with $10,000 already awarded me for study in Germany, ready to be deposited in monthly increments in a German bank account, a year of German language behind me, and nowhere to go in Germany?! What in the world, God? What now? I was completely at a loss. No understanding whatsoever. I found myself barely treading water in a sea of uncertainty — a true stretch of my faith. I really had no idea what to do next — the doors all around seemed closed.

Amazingly enough (!), literally within days of this news I had a conversation with a colleague who told me of an Israeli teacher now teaching in Graz, Austria. They did speak German there, right? Germany — Austria. Basically the same thing. (I soon learned NOT to say that out loud! It's like saying to a Canadian they are the same as an American! Oy!)

I had played for this teacher some years before in a master class at NEC. It had been a really good experience. The situation suddenly presented itself as a door that might possibly be opening. It was a long shot, but I contacted him, and he invited me to come and audition for him in Minneapolis while he was there. I started making phone calls and travel arrangements, and in what seemed like a few days I was once again on a plane, wondering at what God was planning. I stayed with a friend who was living in Minneapolis and then had my audition.

The whole trip is now a bit of a blur (except for my excursion to the Mall of America!). But on my return a few days later, after having been told by this professor that he had accepted me for study, I slowly started to see the pieces of the puzzle fall into place again — God's picture this time, not mine. I called the Beebe Grant committee, explained the situation, and was again amazed as they immediately replied that it would be no problem to switch countries. Faxes were flying all over the world (the pre-email era!), the last from this professor informing me that it would be much easier from a paper-work angle if I would study with him privately in Vienna, instead of at the university in Graz. I figured if I was going to be forced into being in the classical music center of the world, I'd have to comply! I was thrilled! All the arrangements were made, and I found myself looking forward to walking in the steps of the greatest musicians the world has ever known. Vienna.

One thing was certain: I was no longer in control! God was doing it all. Having watched as doors had opened, then closed, then as others had opened in a different direction, or at least in an utterly unexpected way, I was beginning to understand that God had *His* purpose, which was far beyond my comprehension, let alone anything I could ever have imagined. When all was said and done, I knew God had moved me, step by step, into exactly the place I was supposed to be. Little did I know then how significant that would really be. At that point, I was content to know that I was in His will, following where He was so clearly leading.

After more phone calls, I was becoming an expert at making travel plans. However, this time buying a ticket which had an open-end return date for up to 12 months later had a very different feel to it! Reality kicked in as I held that ticket in my hand—and even more as I watched the first major chunk of my grant money disappear into some airline bank account! September found me sorting through clothes, books and music—once again trying to figure out how to pack a year's worth of living in a foreign country, of whose climate and culture I knew nothing, into the ever smaller two suitcases.

However, there was one thing I did know. Like Moses before setting off on the journey to the Promised Land, if God's presence wasn't going with me, I wasn't going anywhere! Yet, even though I didn't have a cloud by day and a pillar of fire by night, I was certain that God was directing my own journey.

There came with all of these developments that peace that passes understanding — basically, that we as humans can't explain! I certainly couldn't have given anyone any logical explanation. But at that point, the cloud couldn't have been clearer, nor the pillar of fire brighter. God was leading. I would follow. Even to the other side of the world, or as the British affectionately refer to the Atlantic Ocean — "across the pond."

Saviour, Like a Shepherd Lead Us

Dorothy A. Thrupp, 1936

Saviour, like a Shepherd lead us;
Much we need Thy tender care.
In thy pleasant pastures feed us;
For our use Thy folds prepare.
Blessed Jesus, Blessed Jesus,
Thou hast bought us, Thine we are
Blessed Jesus, Blessed Jesus,
Thou hast bought us, Thine we are

We are Thine; do Thou befriend us.
Be the Guardian of our way;
Keep Thy flock, from sin defend us;
Seek us when we go astray.
Blessed Jesus, Blessed Jesus,
Hear Thy children when we pray;
Blessed Jesus, Blessed Jesus,
Hear Thy children when we pray;

Early let us seek Thy favour;
Early let us do Thy will.
Blessed Lord and only Saviour,
With Thy love our bosoms fill.
Blessed Jesus, Blessed Jesus,
Thou hast loved us; love us still.
Blessed Jesus, Blessed Jesus,
Thou hast loved us; love us still.

Where you go I will go, and where you stay I will stay. Your people will be my people and your God my God.
                                                    Ruth 1:16

4
Saviour, Like a Shepherd Lead Us
A companion for the journey

The automatic doors swung open, and suddenly before me was a sea of foreign faces, restrained only by the low bars on which they were leaning and the DO NOT ENTER signs on the doors through which I had just come. That nervous feeling in the pit of my stomach accompanied me as I stepped over the threshold of the safe and noncommittal world of travel and beyond the point of no return.

As the doors closed behind me, that forbidding DO NOT ENTER now made my only available course straight into the unchartered waters before me. Pushing my cart of violin-topped suitcases like a shield in front of me, I scanned the faces, knowing I would recognize no one, but hoping for something—anything. And there it was. Leaning nonchalantly on the bars—the typical posture for an airport arrivals wait, unpredictable in length—was a man holding a piece of paper on which was written, "Starla Joy Nelson." I don't know that I've ever been so happy to see my own name in ink!

The one bringing such relief was Omar Beiler, pastor of the international Assemblies of God church in Vienna. My dad had contacted him, prompted by that paternal concern of his little girl going across the world to a strange city where she knew no one. At that moment I was extremely grateful for that intervention! I made my way over to the man in question, and identified myself with the sign in his hand.

Before long I found myself being driven into Vienna and trying to come to grips with the fact that I was here. As we crossed over the Danube, I wondered how in the world Strauss came up with the title "The Beautiful Blue Danube." What I was seeing was definitely not blue, and beautiful was also a bit of a stretch. I would learn later that what I had crossed was only a small branch off the river that ran through the city, and that the real Danube just a few miles upriver more than earned the name!

We arrived at my hotel, and Omar informed me that he would pick me up at 7 p.m. for a mid-week house group that met at his home. There I would have a chance to meet some people, and it would also make me get up from a nap so I would get over jet-lag more quickly. I agreed. Indeed at that moment, I was too tired and excited to even think about it. So, after falling asleep and forcing myself up a couple of hours later, I managed to get myself out of that crossing-too-many-time-zones drugged state and be ready for the evening.

Omar and Pat made me feel so welcome in their beautiful apartment, and I met some wonderful people that first evening. We talked, had a Bible study and worshipped together—the singing led by a guy about my age who mentioned a fiancée in the U.S. It was an altogether pleasant first evening in Austria. I was at the time completely unaware of the significance those moments would come to have to me.

38

An entry in my journal last year brought that evening back to memory....

"2 October 2008

"A week later, the petals still look like velvet. 12 long-stem red roses — one for each year Chris and I have known each other. He came home with them the other day — September 25. The day I arrived in Vienna, and the day we first met. At the time, in 1996, that God-planned moment was just an insignificant introduction on an extremely significant day. A whole new world had been thrust upon me. Little did I know at that moment that this world I had willingly stumbled into would one day be an integral part of who I would become."

When I tell our story, beginning with the fact that we met my first day in Vienna, I am inevitably asked if it was love at first sight. The answer is a definite no (see above-mentioned fiancée). He was attached, as was I, having a pretty fixed picture of what my life would look like after my 1-year European parentheses. And so Chris and I became friends, enjoying Vienna with a group of 20-somethings, including my roommate and some other friends from the church. Together we went to concerts, operas and restaurants, every time finding another reason to fall in love with this wonderful, magical city.

All this while, with people all around, I was developing a deep respect for this Austrian-Brit who was, above all else, fully committed to and on fire for God. I sensed in him a heart of worship and a desire to do God's will no matter what. And not only that, he was the first guy I'd ever met who, like my father, not only opened the door for a lady, but also made sure he was walking on the outside of the sidewalk. I had assumed that aspect of gentlemanly conduct had been forgotten after my dad's generation!

All that to say—and no one ever believes this part of the story, 'though it's true—there was no romantic interest for either of us. (Chris has told me since, though, that he did think I was beautiful when I first walked into that house group...sigh....) We became good friends, finding we had a lot in common, from classical music (he played the cello) to world views to our mutual love for the Lord and our desire to serve Him. I found myself thinking the girl in America wearing his ring would be very blessed to have such a man standing by her. He was completely committed to her, even when her situation in the relationship became strained. To make a long story short and slightly less painful, there came a point when the engagement was broken, despite his loyalty and his efforts to maintain his commitment.

Somehow, in all of this, God was showing me what it meant to have someone by your side who would be a godly husband—someone to love and respect completely. I realized anew the importance of having someone who would not only love me, but spur me on in my relationship with the Lord—together drawing closer to Him.

It became clear that interest was developing on both sides, and from then on, things started to change rather quickly. Somewhere in there was an emotional roller coaster of a week, with heartbreak being chased by the excitement of knowing that this was God doing something big. Confirmation came over the phone lines with a parental blessing, never having met Chris, and knowing it might mean life in Austria and not Seattle. Somehow my parents knew that if this was God's plan, it would be right and good. I was in tears, having desperately wanted their approval, and here it was handed to me without question. All of a sudden, I knew I was in the center of God's will, and His hand was guiding me.

He was faithful to shake me out of my own way, showing me that His path was where I really wanted to be after all.

For Chris and me it was clear from the beginning of our relationship that we were not dating to see if this was "it". We knew. God had brought us together in such an incredible way — bringing me from the other side of the world and seeing His leading step by step — there was no question. So, shortly after my parents came to Vienna in April, 1997, to "check him out" as my dad puts it, we were engaged. I couldn't wait to show him off to my family in Seattle that summer. He came to meet everyone, plan the wedding and be there for the engagement party my sister threw for us. He passed the sister test, even though she didn't like the fact that I'd be moving to Austria. At our party she put letters up on the wall saying, "Once upon a time, in a land far, far away…."

Our fairy tale continued on January 10, 1998, when we celebrated our wedding in Seattle. Chris, brave man, met 350 of the 500 people in one afternoon — all with grace and charm, I might add. I was blessed to be able to wear my mom's wedding dress from 1950, and Chris looked every inch the English gentleman. Our fathers performed the ceremony, a reminder of the incredible heritage we've both been given. The music our friends played made the afternoon a concert, and the song, "Saviour, Like a Shepherd Lead Us", breathed the prayer of our hearts. The Norwegian ladies put on a beautiful spread of finger foods that we only ever saw afterwards in the pictures. Our only regret of the day was that we didn't get to eat more than the few bites we fed each other of the incredible chocolate/chocolate mousse wedding cake!

Our honeymoon in South Africa, for the first time taking advantage of the benefits of Chris' job at Austrian Airlines, was an incredible beginning of married life for the two of us. On our return to Vienna we looked forward to my parents' coming to visit us in our new home and celebrate again with our church, Chris' grandmothers and other relatives who were unable to travel to Seattle with the rest of the family. That celebration was a lot of fun, the highlights being Chris' brother Nick's hilarious speech and the African women of the church wrapping a traditional cloth around my wedding dress and trying to get me to dance "African" with them. It at least gave everyone good reason to laugh — including me!

In everything that happened in those months, we were able to clearly see and be in awe of the miracle of how God does things. His faithfulness is so great. And to look back and see how He orchestrated people and circumstances to bring us to that place was and still is one of the most amazing testimonies I can give.

Chris is truly my gift from God. My companion for life's journey. Like Sam is to Frodo in *The Lord of the Rings* — there to encourage, help, strengthen and protect. To laugh and cry with. To walk beside. To pick me up when I fall. To remind me again and again that God is faithful.

This is my husband. "This is my lover, this is my friend." (Song of Solomon 5:16)

> Saviour, like a shepherd lead us.
> Be the guardian of our way.
> Thine we are.

I Need Thee Every Hour

Annie S. Hawks & Robert Lowry, 1872

I need Thee ev'ry hour, most gracious Lord
No tender voice like Thine can peace afford

I need Thee, oh, I need Thee;
Ev'ry hour I need Thee!
Oh, bless me now, my Saviour;
I come to Thee!

I need Thee ev'ry hour, stay Thou nearby.
Temptations lose their pow'r when Thou art nigh.

I need Thee ev'ry hour, in joy or pain;
Come quickly and abide, or life is vain.

I need Thee ev'ry hour, most Holy One.
Oh, make me Thine indeed, Thou blessed Son!

Morning, noon, and night I cry out in my distress, and the Lord hears my voice.

Psalm 55:17

5
I Need Thee Every Hour
Especially at 4:30 a.m.

My sister could have made a fortune. I'm sure some greeting card company would have paid big money for what I'm certain would have been a best-selling welcome-to-motherhood card. The scene was perfect for it: Christmas decorations beautifully hung, yet unnoticeable because of the mounds of laundry covering the living room, a frazzled mom with hair in curlers bending over the ironing board, arms awkwardly outstretched so as not to disturb the baby sleeping in the carrier attached in front of her, ironing the umpteenth shirt from the pile behind her.

Victoria had captured the moment, managing a steady hand to shoot the picture while shaking with laughter—at my expense! You'd think my own sister would have had a bit more compassion, but no—she was having too much fun making a mockery of my misery! She had come for a holiday visit—not to see me (ha!), but to see David, our wonderful little baby boy. He was born on October 26, 2001—Austria's national holiday—and had brought much joy to our home, not to mention some chaos and not a few sleepless nights!

The three and a half years up to that point had been filled with so many experiences. Married life had proven to be wonderful. And like any new stage of life, there had been adjustments to be made—new things to get used to. Add to that, which is normal for all newlyweds, setting up house in a new country. My list of new experiences included things like cooking dishes without cans of cream of mushroom soup (it is possible, I've found!), shopping for toothpicks without any idea of what they are called in German (who thought to look in the toothbrush section—they're for testing cakes, aren't they?!), drying clothes on a rack in the dining room and living quite happily like every other Austrian—without a dryer. On top of that, I now had a British mother-in-law who said that a sweatshirt is a sweater, a sweater is a jumper and a jumper is a pinafore. Not to mention cookies vs. biscuits, and tom*a*to vs. tom*aah*to!

However, despite all of the changes I'd experienced, marriage was more fun than I'd ever dreamed. And now we had embarked on the greatest adventure of all: children! (Add to my list of experiences: childbirth in German. Probably good that I will most likely never have a baby in the States—I would have no idea what anything is called in English!)

David was making everything fun, and we were happy, albeit somewhat tired. Life was completely different for both Chris and myself, which I knew was to be expected. I even expected the nights to be what they were—short and not always so sweet. I went through the time when David wouldn't go back to sleep after nursing in the night, and I spent 2 hours walking and rocking him until he would finally doze off again. As a first-time mom who didn't know any better, letting him cry it out was unheard-of.

I have to say, though, my prayer life took on a whole new dimension. I would spend those two hours in the middle of the night walking and looking at our family picture wall, praying for everyone on it. I was so tired if I didn't pray I would have cried, I think! The evenings were the same. When he was nine months old we finally quit dancing him to sleep in the evening. A good night had taken 2-3 songs on the Steven Curtis Chapman CD — a bad night was the whole CD and one or two exhausted parents. Remember, this was baby number one — Rebekah didn't get this luxury. We had learned something. We put her to bed, gave her a kiss and walked out of the room. It worked just fine!

All of this hadn't really surprised me in our parental adventure. However, what I wasn't quite prepared for was the phase David went through at about 14 months old. He would wake up at 4:30 a.m., happy, talkative and completely ready for the day. And there was no convincing him to go back to sleep. I would stumble around the apartment, get him some breakfast by moonlight — not as romantic as it sounds — and try to somehow stay awake enough to make sure he didn't get into any trouble. Hours later when he finally fell asleep for a nap, I would most often crash on the couch, trying to somehow catch up to his energy level. I never did. I still haven't.

Probably one of my biggest lessons in God's faithfulness came during this time. The obvious one was that God gives us the strength we need to make it through the day. But one evening I learned in a very real way that He is always in control, and He will never leave us alone.

It was a typical Wednesday evening at our apartment. There were about 15 people milling about, some chatting in the living room, some preparing food in the kitchen. We were about to start our weekly church house group meeting when I heard David cry a bit in his sleep. Normally I would have waited to see if it continued and then let him be. But that morning he had thrown up and hadn't been feeling too great all day. So I went in to check on him.

I'll never forget that moment as long as I live. I walked over to his crib and in the semi-darkness I saw him shaking violently. I quickly turned the light on and turned to him again. He stopped shaking and lay completely limp. His eyes rolled back into his head and he looked completely lifeless. I screamed for Chris to come and started sobbing uncontrollably. Chris came running and immediately kicked into survival mode.

I've learned one difference between men and women. Whereas we tend to go into an emotional frenzy, which is exactly what was happening to me, men seem to somehow be able to be completely practical and then have their collapse later. Chris picked David up, shouted to the group standing in shock in the living room to start praying, and all his first aid and medical training instincts took over.

David started breathing a lifetime later—okay, maybe it was a minute or so. He was still limp and unresponsive, but alive, which is more than he looked two minutes earlier. Chris took him out of the room and called the hospital, while I sat down on a chair and sobbed hysterically in relief and fear simultaneously. I don't even know if I even thought to pray. But God knew my heart, my desperation, and heard it for the cry it was. About 10 minutes later we were on our way to the hospital, leaving our friends in our apartment to have the meeting without us, or whatever they did. I don't really know.

When we arrived at the hospital, they looked at David and calmly informed us that he had most likely had a febrile convulsion—as if this happened all the time. We were to later learn that it does happen all the time, when a fever shoots up too quickly, more often with boys than girls, and that 98% of the time it is completely harmless. However, it is true that if you don't know what's happening, it looks absolutely terrifying. Actually, even when you do know, it still looks

48

horrendous, as we were to find out 4 more times over the next few years.

As a routine procedure, the nurses prepared to insert a catheter in David's arm in case intravenous medication was needed. By this time he was beginning to respond normally, and I held him on the table as they approached with the needle. I turned my head away, and as they tried unsuccessfully to find a vein, my tears ran down my cheeks as my little boy screamed in pain and terror. After 10 minutes of poking around, they decided to try the other arm. Five minutes later Chris had had enough. He told them to stop. He would take responsibility for not having the IV in place.

It was a nightmare. And from the trauma of that awful night, David developed an absolute dread of all things medical, and he's had more than his share of experiences. Even now, the thought of turning 10 is filled with negative anticipation, just because when he was 5 and had a tick shot (routine here in Austria), we told him during his screams that he wouldn't have to have another for 5 years. So much for saying something that you think will be forgotten when the moment passes.

David and I were admitted to the hospital, where the children's ward was filled to capacity. They put a crib in the waiting room and I sat in a chair. He was to stay until the fever was gone completely. Chris and I slowly recovered from the events of the evening, and seeing David back to his normal happy self the next morning was one of the greatest reasons for thanksgiving I've ever experienced. Chris brought me what I needed to stay in the hospital, where we were for two more nights.

Well, remember that this was during David's 4:30 a.m. phase? Imagine that in a hospital hallway, with a 14-month-old walking bundle of ceaseless energy, and even the newborn babies respectfully adhering to civil hours of waking

49

and sleeping. We spent a lot of time running up and down the hall, then back to our waiting room post. At 4:30 a.m. when I went to the nurse to ask for some cereal to give David for breakfast, she looked at me like I was insane, and said, "It's 4:30 in the morning!" As if I didn't know. I tried to smile sweetly, although that wore off pretty quickly when it really appeared that in her disbelief she wasn't going to give me anything. I wanted to tell her that she could be the one to tell David that "nothing happens in this ward before 7 o'clock." I'm sure he would have taken it well from her. We eventually got some breakfast, and 2 days later, I was never so glad to go home from anywhere.

Through all of this, God was with us. Especially looking back on those moments, we can see His faithfulness to keep us and watch over us, despite our fear and human reactions — maybe even because of that fear. He doesn't expect us to be super-spiritual and unemotional when tragedy strikes. All one has to do is look at the Psalms and see King David sinking in the mire or ranting about his enemies or soaking his pillow with tears. Yet God calls him a man after His own heart.

A friend once said to me that it's okay to vent our emotions to God — He can handle it! Because in the midst of all our tear-spilling and anger-letting and desperate conversations (usually one-sided!) with God, He doesn't wonder at our lack of faith. He just listens, waiting for us to come to the point of being ready to listen. Then He offers a love and a comfort and a reason to trust Him. All we have to do is remember His faithfulness in times past. That whole experience with David became yet another part of my faithful God story — something I could look back on when the next trial came along — which it did, again and again. And I know that when the next trial comes, the same Father who held us then will hold us again.

So though I may panic, go into hysterics, drown in a pool of tears or stumble under the emotional weight of whatever life might bring me, I need not despair. For in the words of Marilla in *Anne of Green Gables* (a great source of wisdom — or at least great lines!), "To despair is to turn your back on God." Having seen His faithfulness, there is no question of that, even in the worst of situations. Because I know that I know that I know I can trust Him. He has never failed, nor will He ever. And so whatever the need and *whenever* the need, whether in the night, or at 4:30 in the morning, or most likely *every* hour, He is there. Faithful. Always.

Just as I Am

Charlotte Elliott, 1835

Just as I am, without one plea
But that Thy blood was shed for me,
And that Thou bidd'st me come to Thee,
O Lamb of God, I come! I come!

Just as I am, and waiting not
To rid my soul of one dark blot,
To Thee whose blood can cleanse each spot,
O Lamb of God, I come! I come!

Just as I am, tho' tossed about
With many a conflict, many a doubt,
Fightings and fears within, without,
O Lamb of God, I come! I come!

Just as I am — Thou wilt receive,
Wilt welcome, pardon, cleanse, relieve;
Because Thy promise I believe,
O Lamb of God, I come! I come!

Just as I am! Thy love unknown
Hath broken ev'ry barrier down;
Now to be Thine, yea, Thine alone,
O Lamb of God, I come! I come!

O LORD, you have searched me and you know me. You know when I sit and when I rise; you perceive my thoughts from afar. You discern my going out and my lying down; you are familiar with all my ways. Before a word is on my tongue you know it completely, O LORD.

Psalm 139:1-4

6

Just as I Am
With ketchup in my eyes

A few years ago I lead a Bible study on the names of God. One of His names is *El Roi* — "the One who sees." And no, I didn't remember that off the top of my head. I had to go to David's room to look it up on the children's church craft we did on the names of God, now hanging on his closet. My memory used to be better....

Anyway, that name is the one that probably means the most to me. He sees me. When I look good, and when I don't — inside or out. When I'm on top of the world, and when I have to scrape myself up off the floor. When I preach a sermon, and when I shout at my children. When I'm totally on fire for Him, and when my Bible sits with a layer of dust, waiting for me to make the time to sit at His feet and listen. Knowing that He sees all that and loves me in spite of it all is one of the greatest comforts — one of the most amazing truths I can imagine.

There was one season of my life when the comfort of knowing *El Roi* was probably the most needed. It started the day our first daughter was born. No...before that. I had had an incredibly rough pregnancy. I wasn't on bed-rest or anything like that. It was just 4 months of queasiness — trying to play with 1½ -year-old David while trying to stay horizontal on the couch — and then 1 month of mostly okay, and then 4 months of Braxton Hicks contractions which became quite painful in the last month. Throughout I had horrible back pain and those pains that shoot down into the leg.

After false labor and a fruitless trip to the hospital one day before she was due, followed by 4 hours of contractions every afternoon, she came a week late. That was one of the greatest days of my life — partly because the pregnancy was over! But as any mother will tell you, it was mostly because I really did get to participate in a miracle — for the second time, and I even found a few moments to document it....

"1 October 2003

"Today our little Rebekah Joy was born! We got to the hospital at 9:15 [a.m.] and an hour later we had a daughter! It went so quickly, after so many weeks — months — of contractions, the last 2 weeks being extremely uncomfortable. But now she's here, and she's beautiful... I'm so grateful for our little daughter. God has blessed us so much. Rebekah has a lot of brown hair — at the moment, anyway — and I can't really tell her eye color yet. But she is so sweet. Lord, thank You for Rebekah. Let Your hand rest on her, and may she truly become a beautiful woman of God — and a joy to You.

"The midwife was wonderful, and called us both Joy, because she loved the name. Our girl is

54

already a joy to us, and with David, our wonderful boy, we are the happiest of parents.

"Rebekah was a week late, and it was an extremely frustrating week for us. A stretch of our faith and trust. And I'm not sure we did so well. But just yesterday I read in Philippians about our attitude being that of Jesus, and to do everything without complaining. It was a timely reminder to me that my attitude was a choice. Thank you, Lord, for that lesson, and at that time. Remind me of that in the days to come — with 2 children and more challenges. You will be the strength of my heart and my portion forever."

God truly has been my strength and portion. However, when I wrote those words, I think I had no idea how much I would need it. Probably the most telling of all is that the next entry in my journal was almost 2 years later! Life changed drastically that day, though I didn't realize it until I left the hospital 3 days later. (That was early here in Austria — you can stay 5 days if you want to.)

Chris and I brought our little bundle of joy home, and she promptly started screaming.

For 3 months.

Except when she ate or slept. I've heard of babies who scream for 9 months. I don't know how those parents survive without ending up in jail for unmentionable crimes.

We were beside ourselves. I honestly don't know how we would have made it without God and each other. When one of us couldn't take it anymore, we would shove her into the other's arms and go into another room and shut the door so we wouldn't throw her out the window.

As I write that it sounds absolutely ghastly, but that's how it was, as much as I don't want to put it in print. Those were days when we questioned God, faith, prayer,

55

everything—you name it. But what else is there? We either come to God even in the worst of times, when it seems He is silent, or we turn away. But where else would we go? I know—even in the worst of times—that He is good. He is true. He is faithful. So there's no other choice but to get through it. And we did.

Rebekah did stop crying. And she became a happy, wonderful baby who truly made our home a place of joy. The transformation was really unbelievable. You can even see the difference in her face in photos, seemingly from one day to the next. We still can remember those first months. However, the memory of the nightmarish emotions elicited during that season has faded in light of the fun and happiness the succeeding years have brought. I can't imagine life without our sweet Rebekah. She is a gift from heaven.

There were times during those first 2 years with a baby and a toddler when I thought I would just give up. It's tough. Fun, sometimes—but let's face it, really hard. Life consists of diapers, burp cloths, diapers, cleaning up messes, diapers, eating meals cold, diapers, Old MacDonald Had a Farm, diapers, cleaning up messes, diapers, playgrounds, diapers, Bob the Builder, and diapers. Oh, and diapers.

I remember many, many days when I was still in my robe at 10 a.m.—or later—hoping the mailman wouldn't ring the bell and I'd have to go to the door. I remember trying to put on a brave smile when Chris left the apartment at 7:30 in the morning to go to work, knowing I'd be on my own for 10 or more hours, wondering what in the world I would do with 2 small children to make the time go by.

I don't know what I would've done without friends like Lisa and Christine, who were in the same boat. We would meet just to see another big-person face, and maybe have 2 minutes—if we were lucky—of adult conversation. But just knowing there was someone who understood was enough.

Someone who understood that a one-sentence prayer conveyed a thousand thoughts coming from deep within. Someone who understood that finding time to read the mail, let alone the Bible, was a sometimes insurmountable challenge. It was enough knowing we were in this together. With each other, and with God.

It was during this 2-year period, when my journal sat empty except for a few to-do lists, packing lists, and things-to-get-in-Seattle lists, that I had a particularly ridiculous morning. I even realized how absurd it was when it happened, because I knew I had to write it down. David was almost 3 and Rebekah almost 1. That morning's episode proceeded as follows:

"Tuesday, September 27, 2004

"*Events between 9 & 10:30 a.m.*

- David wants to go without diaper, so I give him underwear. He is back & forth to toilet 10 or more times — goes once.
- Phone rings — Aniko [doctor friend] to ask about [my] tick shot yesterday, I tell her about pain in leg. She gives me # of doctor friend.
- Start to take shower, hear Rebekah screaming. David has run over her foot with riding car.
- Both kids screaming. Phone rings. Nina. Schedule house party.
- Rebekah with video. Try shower again. David starts screaming. Get out to find him standing in puddle. Get him in bath.
- Clean puddle. Phone rings. Aniko has called Dr. friend & described symptoms. I probably have shingles. Need to go to doctor ASAP.

- Get dressed. Go to bathroom as David dumps 2 cups of water on rug and floor [after having been told not to]. I step in water with both socks. I lose it. David gets spanking. I clean up floor.
- Try to calm down & comfort David. He asks what's the matter & says I have ketchup in my eyes (because they're red from crying)."

I'll never forget that morning. Not that any of the above was atypical for any given day. It was just because it all happened within a 1½ hour period! Crazy. It might have been the first time David consciously recognized my red eyes (as I've said before—it's stupidly obvious when I've been crying), but it would definitely not be the last he would see of my tears.

Sometimes I wish I could blame ketchup, or onions, at least! But usually it's because either a) God has been speaking to me, and it's my response—those are good tears! Or b) I'm totally overwhelmed with life—again. Too often it's b). But even then, God sees. He is *El Roi*. He sees, and He cares, and He loves. And I can come to Him—just as I am.

Even with ketchup in my eyes.

Sweet Hour of Prayer
William W. Walford, 1845

Sweet hour of prayer, sweet hour of prayer,
That calls me from a world of care
And bids me at my Father's throne
Make all my wants and wishes known!
In seasons of distress and grief
My soul has often found relief,
And oft escaped the tempter's snare,
By thy return, sweet hour of prayer-

Sweet hour of prayer, sweet hour of prayer,
The joy I feel, the bliss I share,
Of those whose anxious spirits burn
With strong desires for thy return!
With such I hasten to the place
Where God, my Saviour, shows His face
And gladly take my station there,
And wait for thee, sweet hour of prayer.

Sweet hour of prayer, sweet hour of prayer,
Thy wings shall my petition bear
To Him whose truth and faithfulness
Engage the waiting soul to bless;
And since He bids me seek His face,
Believe His word, and trust His grace,
I'll cast on Him my ev'ry care,
And wait for thee, sweet hour of prayer.

What other nation is so great as to have their gods near them the way the Lord our God is near us whenever we pray to him?
Deuteronomy 4:7

7

Sweet Hour of Prayer
Or at least 2 minutes

It's the strangest feeling. I'm writing this on an airplane. There's a big person on my left, another big person on my right, and the only little person to be seen is across the aisle and up a row, and I've never seen him before, nor am I responsible for him.

No one is asking me for more juice. No one is asking me when we are going to get there. No one is needing me to chase them up and down the length of the plane for the tenth time. I have one small purse as hand luggage. No diaper bag. No extra wipees. No food supply in case what is offered is yucky. Like I said, it's the strangest feeling.

Chris and I are off to England for a leadership conference. The kids are with Chris' parents for 4 days and 3 nights, and we are free to take in as much as we can with no distractions. It is an incredible gift! I'm not exactly sure how to act. I keep thinking I'm forgetting something. But, no. Here we are, and I'm actually writing! In the middle of the day! Unbelievable.

This comes as a much-needed break from routine. Last week was the first week of summer vacation from school. Although I think maybe that should be re-named somehow. Vacation for the kids, maybe. I feel like my workload doubled, at least! The "sweet hour" of prayer is anyway just a nice line in a hymn—now even the 2 minutes have become a luxury.

But I have learned something in this season of life. Prayer is communication with God, and whether I spend it in a quiet place or in conversation with Him while folding the laundry or washing the dishes (especially when the dishwasher breaks!), the most important thing is that it is a 2-way dialogue, where I am quiet enough (at least in my spirit!) to listen. My tendency is to deliver a monologue with a list of my needs and forget that He wants relationship with *me*. Amazing.

It is so easy as a Christian mom to fall under a mass amount of guilt. We hear of the incredible times of prayer and worship that those around us in the church are having, and we fall into spiritual depression because of our struggle to find any time to sit and read our Bibles or pray. Or when we finally find a minute to do so at the end of the day, we fall asleep after reading, "Jesus said unto His disciples…."

One of the most encouraging things I've heard as a mom was when my friend, Vicki Harris, was praying for me. She's an incredible woman of prayer, and raised 3 children as a single parent. She prayed that when the times came when I hadn't read my Bible in 5 days (upon which I immediately started crying…yes, again! It was as if she could read my very thoughts!), God would bring His Word to my mind, because for my whole life I have stored the Scriptures in my heart. It is there, and when I need it, it will come.

That was such a freeing moment in my spiritual life. God is not sitting up in heaven frowning at us when another day goes by and we haven't spent an hour on our knees. He is kneeling beside us as we put a bandage on an owie, or preparing yet another snack for the boy with the bottomless pit in his stomach.

I have learned the importance of having Scripture become internalized, because if it is there, I can retrieve it in a moment of despair or uncertainty. That's why I have started to put verses on bits of paper in various places, especially the inside of the bathroom door, where I might actually have 10 seconds of privacy to read something!

I am learning to *live* in a conversation with God, not just rely on specific times spent in focused prayer, as important as that is. When we can't manage that, we need to have as a basis a friendship with Jesus, lived out in the midst of our everyday lives. God is a God of love, and He wants *relationship* with us. Not religion or rules.

All that to say, there's a very clear picture that keeps coming to mind. I see myself as a girl, then as a teenager, kneeling at the front of my dad's church on the steps to the platform, or in the front row, made easier on the knees when the new red carpet went all the way under the pews.

I see the tears running down my cheeks as the hunger of my heart as a young girl is met by Jesus at my side, filling me with His Holy Spirit. Again and again. All those Sunday nights when we sought Him for more, coming to the altar in constant surrender. I see it now as an integral part of what God continues to do in me—to stir in me. That was the beginning, the foundation. And He continues building.

There is one moment in time that stands out to me as a huge milestone in my spiritual journey. I will never forget it. It was the year before David was born. We were in Pensacola, Florida, where we were visiting friends whom we had met in Vienna when they came from the Pensacola revival to do a worship seminar week at our church. Bill & Lisa Ancira had come with their boys, leading the team.

Chris was so hungry for more of what we had seen in Bill and Lisa and the rest of the team — a fire and a passion for whatever God had to offer. My desire was also for more, but I did not want to look like I was "chasing after" revival, reasoning that God could do the same thing at home in Vienna. So as far as I was concerned, we were in Florida just to visit friends, and we went to the revival meetings since we were there anyway.

What I had yet to learn was that, yes, God *can* do anywhere what He does in places where there is an outpouring of His Spirit. And He does. However, He also honors the hungry heart that goes searching for the treasure, not giving up until it is found.

And so we were in Pensacola, and I was resisting giving in completely to whatever the Holy Spirit wanted to do, afraid of what it might look like. Looking back, my logic or reasoning seems completely upside down. But I also know that it was a process — a part of my spiritual development and growth.

I can remember sitting on the bed in the home of our friends and hosts, Mark & Kim, listening to the new Steven Curtis Chapman CD that Chris had just bought (the one that would later be used to dance David to sleep!). There was a song about coming to God with great expectations. I sat there, and suddenly I knew I had a choice. I could either see this trip as simply a fun time of vacation, or I could let God in, and let Him do *whatever* He wanted in me, no matter how strange it might feel at first, and it would be an incredible leap forward in my relationship with Him.

I can remember finally coming to a point of surrender, letting my hunger for Him overtake my mind's need for understanding and propriety. As I made that conscious decision, there were no fireworks, no visions of glory — just a peace that came with knowing I could trust Him with every part of my life, my emotions, my heart. From that point on, it was no longer just a vacation. It was an awesome display of God's love for me, of His power, and of what can happen when He shows up in a place — in a life.

That was definitely a turning point for me. There have still been highs and lows. Mountain top experiences and valleys of discouragement and the testing of trust. But I think I can honestly say that I've never doubted Him, although I often don't understand His ways. I have seen His faithfulness over and over. Even in my stubbornness and failings. His love for me keeps drawing me deeper and deeper in to the awesome security of being His child. And He has *so* much more. There's always so much more....

So now as I finish these thoughts on drawing closer to God, the conference in England is over. We have heard men and women of God pour the kingdom of heaven into our hearts. We've had 3 nights of incredible sleep! And now we are going home to our children, our church, our city — excited to see what God will do. The three days of worship and prayer and God's Word to our spirits have been incredible — another filling station on this journey of faith.

Even though I now go home to the craziness of life where worship happens while doing the ironing and the sweet hour of prayer is once again a far-off dream, I know that God sees me. That He knows where I am. And He is right there beside me as I fold the laundry (again) or read a story to my children. And He is pleased with me. He rejoices over me with singing (Zephaniah 3:17).

Sweet hour of prayer? Maybe not today. Maybe not to-morrow. But 2 minutes? Yes, 2 minutes at a time, while walking with Jesus through each and every day.

Faith is the Victory

John Henry Yates, 1891

Encamped along the hills of light,
Ye Christian soldiers, rise,
And press the battle ere the night
Shall veil the glowing skies.
Against the foe in vales below
Let all our strength be hurled.
Faith is the victory, we know,
That overcomes the world.

**Faith is the victory!
Faith is the victory!
Oh, glorious victory
That overcomes the world!**

His banner over us is love,
Our sword the Word of God;
We tread the road the saints above
With shouts of triumph trod.
By faith they, like a whirlwind's breath,
Swept on o'er ev'ry field;
The faith by which they conquered death
Is still our shining shield.

To him that overcomes the foe
White raiment shall be giv'n;
Before the angels he shall know
His name confessed in heav'n.
Then onward from the hills of light,
Our hearts with love aflame;
We'll vanquish all the hosts of night
In Jesus' conqu'ring name.

This is the victory that has overcome the world, even our faith.
1 John 5:4

8
Faith is the Victory
Overcoming my JFK world

Growing up in a world of hymns has given my life a completely different outlook than that of most of my generation. The result is that in any given situation, partial or entire lyrics to the old greats will come to mind, providing exactly the reminder needed at that moment. Since many or most hymns are filled with Scripture, I know that more often than not the phrase going through my head is straight from the Bible, if not pretty close. This was made clear one very long day in New York.

With Chris working for the airline industry, we enjoy the accompanying benefits. Cheap flights are a blessing when family is across the ocean. There is, however, one rather large drawback to this blessing. It is expressed in one word: stand-by. This word has come to elicit in me a sort of silent dread, lurking just below the surface.

On a good day of travel, nothing comes of this feeling—there are seats available on the flight for everyone travelling, and all goes well. Arrival with luggage at the desired destination is a not-to-be-taken-for-granted result. However, on a not-so-good day, this feeling of dread explodes into a what-do-I-do-now hopelessness. I have had these not-so-good days, when there are not enough seats available, and I go back home to wait another day. Or worse, when there are enough seats but no luggage allowed because of too much cargo weight in the plane.

One especially bad day turned out to be the biggest field trip ever to the Copenhagen airport. We arrived without incident and went to catch our connecting flight to Seattle. However, the above scenario ensued, with seats available but too much cargo to allow our luggage to come with us. They could send us to Chicago without any problem, but getting to Seattle from there was *our* problem. We could stay overnight in a Copenhagen hotel and try the same flight the next day, but the likelihood of a repeat performance was too great.

I ended up with two children, a stroller, a violin and a cart full of luggage in the ticket hall crying to Chris on the phone, with no idea what to do. In the end, we decided that I should fly back to Vienna and try again with a different route. The children were small enough that the really cool play plane with a slide down the back and the boat with balls for a sea were enough reason to have endured the trip there and back. I, however, had had enough, and on arriving back home and eventually to Seattle, I figured from then on no bad day could be bad enough to cause another break-down in any future stand-by experiences. That was before JFK.

Experiences like the one related above have reiterated for us the need to check and double-check seat availability on a flight before embarking on any journey. And our next trip to Seattle was no exception. The flight looked great—through New York on our airline and on to Seattle from there. No problem. We arrived at JFK having had no incident, and after going through customs we took the sky train (for the children, the best part of the trip!) to the next terminal. I walked confidently up to the gate, only to see on the screen that it did not look good for stand-by passengers.

To make a long story not quite so long, we didn't make it. But there was another possibility just a couple hours later. By this time, however, my confidence was beginning to waver. I learned that it was the Wednesday before Memorial Day weekend, which had escaped me, living in Europe and having enough to do to keep track of Austrian holidays (which are many, and stores are closed, so if you forget and don't go shopping, you eat whatever they have in the freezer section at the gas station!).

Every flight from anywhere going to the west coast was full. If I didn't get on this flight, my chances of getting out of New York before the following Tuesday were getting slimmer as the hours passed. Well, we didn't make it. By this time, I had two children who were so whacked out with the time change they didn't know what was going on.

Somehow I managed to get us to what I thought was a well-known but reasonable hotel, with no luggage, and paying JFK airport hotel prices. That was enough to put me over the edge, until we got there and it turned out to be a really expensive dump. The TV didn't even work, and with the time change we were awake at 2:30 a.m. with the first bus back to the airport at 5 a.m. It was a night never to be forgotten, to be sure.

We had another shot at an 8 a.m. flight the next day. After missing that one, my real break-down occurred. Complete and utter hopelessness reigned. After finally talking with Chris, and somehow hearing his reminder (in his own worry and helplessness) that God is truly in control, David, Rebekah and I started wandering through the terminal, trying to kill another 8 hours until the next flight to Seattle. No great play place with ships and planes and balls was to be seen anywhere.

We finally found in a corner somewhere an old semi-broken slide where much fun could nonetheless be had. I sank down and got out the journal that for whatever reason (!) I had decided to bring along. I started to write, and as I did, God started the miracle. In me.

"24 May 2007

"JFK Airport. 11:38 a.m. Awaiting the flight to Seattle at 4:40 p.m. It will be the fourth attempt to get on a plane in the last 24 hours. I just finished a double chocolate chip frappacino—so good! My attempt, at Chris' encouragement, to find the good in this situation. It did help! The other good is that we found a little play place with a small slide and tunnel—at least something for the children to do. The past 24 hours have been a roller coaster. From confidence to a knot in the stomach. Nervousness to dread. Despair to tears. Completely at a loss to resignation. Only to start the whole thing over again. 3 times. With one dumpy $150 hotel room in between and the only human hope of getting to Seattle anytime in the next 3-5 days lies in the remote possibility of another connecting flight being delayed or a lot of people getting stuck in traffic. Not a confidence-builder. But somewhere deep inside I do know that I have a God—even a Father—who moves far above the realms of human hope, and yes, beyond human understanding. Either He will truly perform a miracle for us here in this melting pot of cultures and human experience, or I will have a choice to learn to trust Him more and keep my cool while all this "worketh patience" in me.

"How much can I handle? I don't know. How many days will these clothes still be fit to wear if the miracle we pray for doesn't happen?! I don't know.

But I do know and choose to stand on His promise that He won't allow more than I can stand. Stand firm. Faith is what overcomes. The victory. Hold on to faith. What I believe. What I know is true. "He who sacrifices thank offerings honors me, and prepares the way that I might show him the salvation of the Lord." Psalm 50 something? Something like that. I will choose to honor You right now. Thank You for this play place and that David and Rebekah are playing so well and are so content. Thank You that for them, our dumpy, expensive motel was an adventure, and sleeping in our underwear was the release of laughter we all so desperately needed. Thank You that after 45 minutes of unsuccessfully attempting to phone Chris today I finally got through. Thank You for friendly ground staff. Thank You that our luggage is in Seattle and not lost somewhere unknown. Thank You that mom and dad were able to get money into the US account in time for me to be able to pay the hotel bill when they didn't accept my non-Visa credit card. Thank You for wisdom in the decision to bring the stroller and not the violin. Thank You for clean sheets and a place to sleep last night. Thank You for wonderful children who have only had meltdowns a couple times. Thank You for the idea to bring this journal so I can record Your faithfulness during these never-to-be-forgotten moments in my life. Thank You for an incredible husband who supports, loves and encourages me in You even from across the ocean. Thank You for friends and family all over the world, some of whom are praying for Your intervention even now. Thank You that Burger King was open before 6 a.m. and that they even had pancakes and apple juice for the children. Thank You that I chose to dress nicely and don't feel like a total frump. Thank You that the black smears on my sweater from the stroller rolling over it outside came out when I washed it. Thank You for these two kids who are playing hide-and-seek with David and Rebekah right now. Thank You for the double chocolate chip frappacino. Thank You for the flight attendant [Chris' colleague] who recognized us as Chris' family on seeing David's face. Thank You for my sweet Rebekah who just shared a big chunk of her cookie with me, and who hugged me and stroked my hair when I cried. Thank You for chases down the moving walkways. Thank You that there was no complaining when there were only pretzels and water and no apple juice in the hotel. Thank You for my little songbirds who sang "Great Is Thy Faithfulness" with me last night before falling asleep. Thank You for this gift of Your perspective of things, larger at this moment than my own. Thank You for this respite in which I can write these thoughts while the children most happily play. Thank You for faith, which truly is my victory that overcomes my JFK world. Thank You for bringing peace to my soul and joy to my heart. There lies, perhaps, the biggest miracle of all."

My lesson was not over, but the miracle had already taken place. God did show Himself when I sacrificed thanks. And to begin with, believe me, it was a sacrifice! I did not feel like it at all. But this verse in Psalm 50:24 came back to me at that moment—a verse that had been made real to me once before. In thankfulness God truly is honored. And in the middle of that airport, while other people's lives swirled around me, God brought my own life to a complete stop in order to remind me again of His great faithfulness.

'Tis So Sweet to Trust in Jesus

Louisa M. R. Stead, 1882

'Tis so sweet to trust in Jesus,
Just to take Him at His word;
Just to rest upon His promise;
Just to know, "Thus saith the Lord."

Jesus , Jesus, how I trust Him!
How I've proved Him o'er and o'er!
Jesus, Jesus, precious Jesus!
Oh, for grace to trust Him more!

Yes, 'tis sweet to trust in Jesus,
Just from sin and self to cease;
Just from Jesus simply taking
Life and rest, and joy and pace.

I'm so glad I learned to trust Him,
Precious Jesus, Savior, Friend;
And I know that He is with me,
Will be with me to the end.

Blessed is the man who trusts in the Lord, whose confidence is in Him.

Jeremiah 17:7

9

'Tis so Sweet to Trust in Jesus

Simple – just not so easy

I've just finished singing this song for David and Rebekah before they went to sleep. They have heard it I don't know how many times. I decided long ago to sing this song for them at bedtime, wanting the importance of it to somehow sink into their very souls. It's a much easier lesson to learn when you're 3 and 5! But it is also one of "life's valuable lessons" that one gets to learn over and over! My enforced visit of the JFK airport was one of those times. My journaling of events continued….

"Later, 3:07 p.m.

"Another 1 ½ hours and we will either be on the 4th plane to Seattle or waiting for number 5.

"I wonder, will I be as strong then as I was after my time of worship in thankfulness this morning? I pray that I will. I'm getting so tired. My eyelids feel like leaden weights every time I blink. To be sure, that is partly caused by the tears shed in my lowest moments today. But I am also simply suffering from jet-lag. Were I in Vienna I could very legitimately go to bed. Or in Seattle I could curl up and take a nap, as Rebekah is doing now in the stroller while David plays with more new friends-for-the-moment. Instead I sit here waiting for the next test. I feel a bit like those times before music history exams at NEC [New England Conservatory], where we had to listen to a perhaps unknown piece then write an essay on it. Maybe not quite as bad, as the end result doesn't depend on my preparation and knowledge or lack thereof! But just the same, the knot is forming, though there is also an underlying peace this time.

"Lord, let Your peace that truly does pass all understanding now guard my heart and mind as I trust in You. 'Tis so sweet to trust in Jesus, just to take Him at His Word. Just to rest upon His promise. Just to know, thus saith the Lord. Jesus, Jesus, how I trust Him. How I've proved Him o'er and o'er. Jesus, Jesus, precious Jesus. O for grace to trust Him more. Great is Your faithfulness. All I have needed, Your hand has provided. This is what I sing to my children every day. Maybe I'm really singing it to myself. It has become and is ever becoming my story, my song. Lord, please let that song still be ringing even if I am there to answer the [pay] phone when Chris calls at 5 p.m. If that is Your plan today, let him hear Your strength in my voice. Let Your strength be made perfect in my weakness. Whatever happens, in everything I will choose to give thanks, for this is Your will. And it is my desire to do Your will. To bring You glory, in my words, thoughts and actions. 'Let the words of my mouth and the meditation of my heart be pleasing in Your sight, O Lord my Rock and my Redeemer.' Psalm 19:14."

"6:55 p.m.

"We are on a plane! Not number 4, but number 5! We didn't make the 4:40 p.m., but I was OK. Chris called at 5 p.m., hoping I wouldn't be there to answer. But I was able to assure him convincingly that I would make it no matter what. I can't express how thankful I am that this "life's valuable lesson" of patience and trust is come to an end! I must admit I don't think I've ever paced as much as the last half hour before I got our seats. We were the last, having seen the last seats go, then at the last second seeing some seats being released again, then being handed the long-awaited magic papers.

"I rejoice and praise the Lord for His goodness, faithfulness and mercy. But most of all I'm so thankful that He took me to a place of worship and gratefulness despite the circumstances. Despite the very real possibility, if not probability, of perhaps days of uncertainty and stress. That place, of gratitude and worship, was my secret place. There I was truly in the shadow and shelter of His wings, protected from despair and dissolution. That little corner of JFK International Airport became the secret place of His presence. The mountain of the Lord—my place of worship. Where God met with me. Thank You, Lord, for Your faithfulness, provision and grace. Thank You, that You love me so much as to reveal a bit more of Yourself to me today, that I might know You more. Remind me again and again of this lesson, and let my heart always be open to Your Spirit's teaching, especially in a time of trial. May I be found faithful. And may I, in everything, give thanks."

I did make it to Seattle that day—day 2, that is. I can truly say I was never so glad to see the back of an airport! And although I never want to do that again, it was worth it. Had I not been able to find the good in that miserable situation—those reasons to be thankful—I think I would have erupted like Mount St. Helens, bringing destruction to myself, my children and anyone in my path! But God was merciful. And I learned—again—how sweet it is to trust in Jesus.

Oh, to Be Like Thee

Thomas O. Chisholm, 1897

Oh, to be like Thee! Blessed Redeemer,
This is my constant longing and prayer.
Gladly I'll forfeit all of earth's treasures,
Jesus, Thy perfect likeness to wear.

Oh, to be like Thee! Oh, to be like Thee,
Blessed Redeemer, pure as Thou art!
Come in Thy sweetness, come in Thy fullness;
Stamp Thine own image deep on my heart.

Oh, to be like Thee! Full of compassion,
Loving, forgiving, tender and kind,
Helping the helpless, cheering the fainting,
Seeking the wand'ring sinner to find.

Oh, to be like Thee! While I am pleading,
Pour out Thy Spirit, fill with Thy love;
Make me a temple meet for Thy dwelling,
Fit me for life and heaven above.

[Jesus said,] I have set you an example that you should do as I have done for you.

John 13:15

10
Oh, to Be Like Thee
I'll let Rebekah do it

This summer we entered a new stage of life and parenting. With David and Rebekah 7 and 5, we realized that we had a decision to make. With 5 years having somewhat faded our memories of Rebekah's first tumultuous months, our adamant unified declaration of never having another baby seemed somewhat exaggerated. But it was not just the passing of time that was changing our mindset. I guess we didn't realize then the joy we would have over the next years, and if we were having so much fun with two children, wouldn't it follow that we would have more fun with more?!

And so one evening this past July, 2009, we put our big kids to bed, and a couple hours later, it was suddenly time to go to the hospital. Two hours later, Miriam Anna was born. It was fast and furious, but she was absolutely beautiful! As the midwife laid her in my arms, my first words were not the rapturous adulations of an adoring parent, I'm sorry to say. Instead, I looked at her perfect little form and said, "Oh my goodness, this is real!"

Somehow with two children at home and life going on in spite of pregnancy, it hadn't completely sunk in that life would be somewhat different after one trip to the hospital. But she is absolutely wonderful, extremely sweet, and all of us, especially big brother and sister, are having so much fun with her. Already she has completely stolen our hearts.

A few weeks ago I was sitting with her in my arms, and as I looked at her, I was reminded of a baby photo of mine. I wondered if she really looked as much like me as I thought. I went to my childhood photo album, and there on the first page was a picture of Miriam. Oh, I mean myself! It was really uncanny. I took the picture and showed it to David who immediately said it was Miriam. Wow. It's amazing how genes work! I knew already that Rebekah had some of me in there, as we'd had the same response with some of her pictures at about 3 years old compared to mine at that age.

Aside from mere physical similarities, it is a known fact that children become like their parents, as my sister likes to point out to me whenever I do something like my mother! But as a parent, that can be a sobering thought. How often have I heard David or Rebekah playing and heard my own words through their mouths. It does make one think a bit about what one says! The truth is, like it or not, and for better or for worse, we are their first example. Enough said.

When David was about 3, he came into the bathroom as Chris was putting on some cologne. He looked up and said, "Smell like Daddy?" Chris bent down and gave him a tiny spray of the scent, and off he went, proud as anything, making all of us smell his chest. It triggered something in Chris, and it became the theme of his next sermon. (What any PK—pastor's kid—knows, is that though your parents really do love you for yourself, what you're really good for is a sermon illustration!)

When we spend time in the presence of our Father, we will start to "smell" like Him. We begin to take on His character, radiating His love to those around us. Just like when I hold Miriam after Chris has cuddled with her. I can smell his cologne and it is good! How God wants us to come close so we can become more like Him—so we can "smell like Daddy."

As a parent, I want my children to become more like Jesus. So if I am the inevitable example to them, I had better make that my goal myself! We each have to make that choice for ourselves, and no matter what our example might be, our children do have to make that choice for themselves as well.

I tried to communicate this to my children one day a few months ago. I was getting myself ready one morning when I heard voices that had been friendly and fun for a long time getting higher and higher in pitch. I intervened before things got out of hand and found the common dispute over the ownership of a certain toy. Trying to remain calm myself, I suddenly had what I thought was a brilliant idea.

I asked them what they thought Jesus would do if he were playing with His brothers or sisters. They hung their heads a bit, though neither was willing to budge at this point. I asked them if they wanted to be like Jesus, which they did, and so I sent them to their rooms and said they could pray and ask Jesus to help them be like Him and show them what He would do.

They went their separate ways without further conflict, and I went to the office to wait for their sure response, quite satisfied with my solution. Some minutes later a quiet and remorseful David came to me at the computer. Silently rejoicing at my victory, I put my arm around him, waiting for him to show God's love to his sister.

He looked at me and said in a quiet voice, "Mommy, I'm gonna let Rebekah be like Jesus." It took a few seconds for his words to sink in. I managed to keep a straight face as I tried to explain how that wasn't exactly what I had in mind, and I sent him back to his room to think again. Later when I could laugh out loud, I realized how smart my son really was—he was going to have that toy no matter what, and if a spiritual answer was what was necessary, then so be it!

I'm not too worried about David! But my prayer for my children is that when a situation calls for a decision or response, they won't wait for the other person to be like Jesus. And if I can be a little bit more like Him myself and get close enough to know what He would do, maybe they will follow my example, and smell that little bit more like Daddy.

The Solid Rock

Edward Mote, c. 1834

My hope is built on nothing less
Than Jesus' blood and righteousness.
I dare not trust the sweetest frame,
But wholly lean on Jesus' name.

**On Christ, the solid Rock, I stand;
All other ground is sinking sand.
All other ground is sinking sand.**

When darkness seems to hide His face,
I rest on His unchanging grace.
In ev'ry high and stormy gale,
My anchor holds within the vale.

His oath, His covenant, His blood
Support me in the whelming flood.
When all around my soul gives way,
He then is all my Hope and Stay.

When He shall come with trumpet sound,
Oh, may I then in Him be found;
Dressed in His righteousness alone,
Faultless to stand before the throne.

By wisdom a house is built, and through understanding it is established; through knowledge its rooms are filled with rare and beautiful treasures.

Proverbs 24:3

11
The Solid Rock
My hope – and house – are built on nothing less

The leaves are almost all blown off the trees. The fiery, brilliant colors of fall are slowly fading. Over the last weeks the hills out my kitchen window have been a beautiful palette of autumn hues, with the vineyards leading up to them an intricate patchwork of color. The image is one that countless artists have attempted to bring alive on canvas, and here it is right out my kitchen window — available for admiration even during the mundane task of washing the dishes.

An inconceivable gift. So undeserved. Even a year and a half after moving in, I am still daily in awe of God's creation, right out my back door. And I am daily grateful. Even now as winter approaches, and autumn loosens its grasp on the beauty of the season, there is one spot of trees on the hills that refuses to let go. All around them the colors have faded, but their bright yellow leaves defy the cold wind, drawing the eye like a light piercing the drabness. When the sun shines, it's as if there's a fire lit where one can draw warmth, sending out an invitation to stop for a moment and rest.

Rest. An interesting word. One which doesn't have a lot of meaning to me sometimes! Considering that this chapter was started about 2 years ago (this is the story of my life — unfinished tasks surround me!), things have changed a bit, and rest has become even more elusive. With a newborn in the house and the beginning of school bringing its yearly chaos, rest seems like a priceless and unattainable luxury!

But there are moments, though they be short-lived, when I sit at the table with the ever-present "cuppa tea" (I did marry a half-Englishman, after all!), and wonder at the home God has given us. We've been here 3 ½ years now, and I still look out the window every day and marvel at the beauty surrounding me.

The fact that we are in this place is a miracle. Chris found the property on the internet, and we set out to explore it. Just outside of Vienna, in Brunn am Gebirge, it sits up on a hill overlooking the city on one side and the Vienna woods on the other. The autobahn/freeway/motorway (pick your country!) is next to the property, though we can't see it from the garden, separated by a noise reduction wall. This brought the price to a third of the rest of the neighborhood and into our range, and after seeing the view, we decided that we would get used to the noise, which can't be any worse than the airplanes that went over our house growing up in Seattle! Driving up the hill to look at the property for the first time, it felt like home before we even got there, and we knew this was the place where God would plant us. It was an incredible gift.

After 3 years of being here, I finally got around to finishing the story of our house in pictures. I put in a frame photos starting with the empty lot and through each building stage up to putting the number 10 on the front of the house. For us it is a reminder of the fun we had in watching it "grow". What a lot of work went into it! At first we watched as someone else put in the hours of physical labor, and brick by brick went up until 4 walls became the promise of something beautiful.

Then *I* watched as Chris put in sweat and tears into tiles and tubs, paint and banisters, floors and baseboards. I should say I watched through modern technology, as Chris sent daily picture updates via email of his progress. I had taken the children to Seattle for 6 weeks while he worked, removing little fingers from big jobs and avoiding weeks of long evenings of Chris wishing he were home with us instead of wrestling with tile cutters and shower basins.

He was amazing—spending the day at work, coming back to his parents' house (where we were living during the building of our house), eating a quick dinner and heading up to our building site to spend the next 4-5 hours working like a fiend. I felt like I was getting the best end of the deal, no work at the house, and visiting my family to boot! But Chris assured me that he was well aware of the work that I was doing with the children on my own, and he constantly reassured me that I didn't need to feel as guilty as I did!

One picture in the frame reminds me of the work that started for me when I returned. In it I am covered in a curtain in the living room. That picture is a story in itself! It all started the year before when my mother-in-law gave me a sewing machine for my birthday. I managed to muster up some excitement and dutifully showed my appreciation for the gift, then asked in a small voice, "Does this mean I have to learn how to use it?!" With somewhat of a laugh in her voice, she answered in a determined, "Yes!" And so I learned. Maybe not with an overwhelming amount of joy, but I did it!

Perhaps the picture that means the most to me, besides seeing 4-year-old David sitting up in the digger truck with the driver and 2-year-old Rebekah sowing grass seed in the yard, is that of our front door. I'll never forget that day. Up to that point the whole project had been our house. Exciting.

Amazing—watching cement, bricks, beams and roof tiles come together to form the structure we had planned on paper. But the day they hung the door on its hinges it became a home.

I was not prepared for the emotions I experienced that day, and the tears that came to my eyes, cheesy as that might be, only reflected my deep gratitude for the faithfulness of God that was represented in that moment. The fact that we were able to buy the property and build the house was only due to His provision.

When the house was finished, Chris and I went through each room, blessing it and dedicating it to the Lord, as well as every person who would pass through its doors. With His wisdom the house had been built, and with His help its rooms would be filled with rare and beautiful treasures. Not just the things, like Chris' great-grandmother's piano, or the violins, or whatever else we might have, treasures though they might be. Instead we would see our home filled with joy, music, worship, memories, friends, and most of all our children, then 2—and now 3—of the most precious treasures one could hope for. Our hope was already built on Jesus Christ, the Solid Rock. Our home would be built on nothing less.

"9 May 2007
"The rain splashing against the window has turned the glass into panes of etched crystal. The darkness of the day—even at mid-morning—makes the room in which I sit that much brighter. It looks cold outside. The wind is blowing the branches of the trees in crazed gyrations, first this way, then that. But the house is warm, and the cup of tea on the table reminds me that all is well. It's a peaceful moment, despite the would-be storm. God is here. He has

provided these four walls where we can close the door on the storms of life and find rest. And when the sun shines again, the door will open to welcome traveler, student, friend, family.

"Lord, thank You for this home. Let it be a place of joy and refuge for my husband, my children, and any person who crosses its threshold. Let it truly be a lighthouse, whose beacon reaches across the rugged coastline of humanity — to bring hope to those who are sinking, to shine Your light to those smothering in darkness, to stand as a symbol of life to all who see its rays, to remind those safe in the harbor of Your faithfulness, and to be a place where the days' journey ends with the joy of home, the knowledge of Your love and the peace of Your presence."

How Firm a Foundation

Attributed to John Keith, 1787

How firm a foundation, ye saints of the Lord,
Is laid for your faith in His excellent word!
What more can He say than to you He hath said —
To you who for refuge to Jesus have fled?

"Fear not, I am with thee, oh, be not dismayed,
For I am thy God, and will still give thee aid;
I'll strengthen thee, help thee, and cause thee to stand,
Upheld by My gracious, omnipotent hand.

"When through the deep waters I call thee to go,
The rivers of sorrow shall not overflow;
For I will be with thee thy trouble to bless,
And sanctify to thee thy deepest distress.

"When through fiery trials thy pathway shall lie,
My grace, all-sufficient, shall be thy supply;
The flame shall not harm thee; I only design
Thy dross to consume and thy gold to refine.

"The soul that on Jesus doth lean for repose,
I will not, I will not, desert to his foes;
That soul, though all hell should endeavor to shake,
I'll never, no never, no never forsake."

In [Christ Jesus] the whole building is joined together and rises to become a holy temple in the Lord. And in him you too are being built together to become a dwelling in which God lives by his Spirit.

Ephesians 2:21, 22

12

How Firm a Foundation

It's the bricks that are sometimes a bit wobbly

There are moments in life which one could replay over and over, and they would never become boring. Events or experiences which, were it possible, we would be more than happy to relive. Places at certain points in our history we would gladly revisit. For me, some of those times would be the thrill of new love, glorious revelations of God's presence and power, magical performances of breathtaking music, a specific moment during the vows at our wedding, the first glimpses of my babies (*after* the birth!), and many more. I think of those times and see God's faithfulness and I am blessed in the remembering.

There are, however, chapters in everyone's stories which would in some ways be better forgotten. Points in times we wouldn't revisit for all the wealth of the world. When I contemplated some of those experiences, I wondered if I could just skip over them in the telling of my life. But I realized, as horrible as they were, they have shaped who I am today. They have taught me much about myself. They have in many cases altered the course of my life. And most of all, they have illuminated perhaps more than anything else the faithfulness of God to me.

One of these occasions was when David stopped breathing. That would probably rate as the most terrifying moment I've ever lived. But that story has already been told. God was faithful, as always, and it was another rung up the ladder of trust.

There is another moment, though, which, when I look back on it, is one of the saddest of all. Not because of what happened to us, but because of where it happened. There is a place which *should* be the safest place on earth. It should be a place where all are welcome, no matter what their situation, status or view of life. It should be a place where prince or beggar can come and find joy, comfort, peace and love beyond measure.

That place should be the church. And I'm not referring to a building. I'm talking about the body of Christ. The people. Christians. Sometimes we do pretty well with being Christ's representatives on earth. Most often, however, on an individual level. Somehow when we come together as two or more, there are often more problems than there is power. We forget that we are supposed to be a family, with Christ as the Head, and instead we become an organization, with a figure at the top to make sure we all are marching to the same orders. Then as soon as one person disagrees with the order-enforcer, that person must go. And in a sad show of extreme disharmony, we go our separate ways, showing the world the opposite of the unity Jesus prayed for.

When I was about 9 or 10 years old, something happened in my dad's church. At the time, I had no idea what was going on. All I knew was that some of my friends were no longer coming to church. I found out years later that there had been lies told about my parents, slanderous letters sent, and hurtful actions which had grievous consequences. And all in the name of—well—I don't really know. Right vs. wrong?

Through the years, and through my own experiences as well as observing others, I have noticed that most of the time divisions occur because someone believes *they* are right, and anyone who disagrees is wrong. But I have to wonder, is it really worth going to war over? With our own church family? Do *we* really have to be the focus? I'm not talking about when someone goes off the deep end with basic foundational beliefs, like Jesus loves us, died for our sins, rose again and sent His Spirit so that we can have relationship with Him. I'm talking about looking to the interest of others, not just to our own (Philippians 2:4). Having the attitude of Jesus, who became a servant—for us!

In any case, in all that happened, I never heard my parents utter a negative word about the people who hurt them. In fact, I didn't really know who had done what, until the last few years when I heard stories about people who had come 20-30 years later to apologize to my mom and dad—some through phone calls, some on their death beds, some when life's experiences had shown them what was really important. Forgiveness had long been given, but their repentance set them free within themselves.

It was this picture of incredible forgiveness, without holding grudges, which came to me some years ago when Chris and I went away from a horrible meeting, which someday I hope to forget. As we walked to the car, tears streamed down my face as I realized we had been, in a matter of hours, stripped of ministry, church family, and in some ways trust in fellow believers. Whether by letter 30 years ago or via email in our time, the damage had been done.

And I now had a choice. To forgive or not to forgive. To let go and learn more about God's grace, or to hold on to bitterness and sink into depression. My parents' experiences and example had taught me. I knew there was no option. As a Christian, I am called to forgive, even as Jesus forgave me. Healing came more slowly, but as I relied more and more on the Healer, crying to Him in my confusion, He showed me the bigger picture. He catches us when we fall. He sees us when we are hurting. And He leads us on into His greater plan.

As I write this, Chris and the two big kids are at church, while I stayed home with a sick Miriam. Our Sunday afternoon service is not something I like to miss. God has brought us to a place where we have learned to trust again. Several years ago, along with Chris' parents and a few others, we felt God leading us to start a church in the city. A place where people can come and know God's love. His healing. His grace. And that place has become family.

They have been there with us through so much these last few years. And their prayers have encouraged us to no end. But what we love the most is the hunger for God that we see week after week. And the love for people, no matter what they look like, no matter what they believe.

We want to see people experience relationship with the One who loves them beyond imagination. And our goal is to have that be more important than everyone agreeing about everything at all times. Because that can never happen. But love beyond boundaries can. And that is our prayer. We enjoy worshipping with other churches, and God is opening doors to do that more and more. It is exciting to see, little by little, the body of Christ functioning together. With Jesus at the head.

As we let the Holy Spirit build us *together*—not where we all agree, but where we all love as Jesus told us to love— the church will become a place where God's presence lives. We will become a place to which people will be drawn—not to a building, but to a family—to us. *We are* the temple of the

Holy Spirit. And when that happens we will see more and more of His glory filling that temple. With Jesus as our cornerstone, and a firm foundation laid according to His Word, maybe it is possible that those wobbly bricks *will* come together to be a beautiful dwelling place for God.

Jesus Will Walk with Me

Haldor Lillenas, 1922

Jesus will walk with me down thru the valley,
Jesus will walk with me over the plain;
When in the shadow or when in the sunshine,
If He goes with me I shall not complain.

**Jesus will walk with me, He will talk with me;
He will walk with me;
In joy or in sorrow, today and tomorrow,
I know He will walk with me.**

Jesus will walk with me when I am tempted,
Giving me strength as my need may demand;
When in affliction His presence is near me,
I am upheld by His almighty hand.

Jesus will walk with me, guarding me ever,
Giving me victory thru storm and thru strife;
He is my Comforter, Counselor, Leader,
Over the uneven journey of life.

Jesus will walk with me in life's fair morning,
And when the shadows of evening must come;
Living or dying, He will not forsake me.
Jesus will walk with me all the way home

[Jesus said,] "...and surely I am with you always...."
Matthew 28:20

13
Jesus Will Walk with Me
In joy and in sorrow

As I write this, Miriam and David are playing together while Rebekah is having her piano lesson. If you were to look at Miriam, you would never know that she is recovering from pneumonia, or that this year she has had five bouts of bronchitis. She appears to be a happy 2-year-old, and it is not at all evident that her bronchial passage is narrower than it should be. You don't see that she has become an expert at inhaling, or that she takes her all-too-familiar medicine willingly — at least most of the time — and especially if there's an audience, even if it's dolls or Lego guys.

This past year has been one that I didn't foresee, which I'm sure is a good thing. I probably would've pushed the fast-forward button had that been an option. But then I would have missed a few things as well. Like the overwhelming feeling of pride as Rebekah sang her solos so beautifully in the choir Christmas program. Or the wonder of finding among his school papers David's incredible drawing of the church in our village. Or the joy of hearing Miriam's sweet words and phrases as her language has developed. But most of all I would have missed experiencing all the times Jesus has walked with me—in joy and in sorrow. I have felt His presence with me more than ever this year, even when I didn't understand—when I questioned Him. And not just because of all that Miriam has gone through this year.

When I considered how I would go about writing this part of my story, I wondered how much I should include. But again I know that all that has happened is now part of who I am—who I am becoming. And it is yet another display of God's faithfulness, whatever the circumstances. So, here it is, some of it best expressed through the thoughts that came in those moments….

"1 April 2011
"When I added this chapter to my list, I imagined the situation in which I would be writing it very differently. As it is, I'm sitting in a hospital bed, watching my roommates eat their lunch, which according to hospital tradition, surely must be bland and completely uninteresting, yet I'm fighting envy. My stomach is growling, but I'm not allowed to eat. I must simply sit and wait for them to come for me, which apparently could be a few more hours.

"I was in a hospital bed to begin with, the day before Thanksgiving last year, when [the above] song came to mind and brought comfort. At that point I was at the end of 3 weeks of uncertainty—hope followed by worry—and finally losing the baby we had so longed for. My plan was to write of my experiences when I had the gift of another baby safely in my arms. Instead, here I am back in the hospital, only to go through it all again. Last week our little one was perfect. At 10 weeks all was well—strong heartbeat and growing beautifully. This week, though, even I could see there was nothing there. What had been clearly a baby in its sweet little gummy bear stage was now just a mass of nothing. Its little heartbeat was no longer with me, but joining the angels in worship before the throne. These two days have been an exercise in trust, learning again that it is an action — a choice — not a feeling. Because I know God is faithful, I know that His plan is bigger than mine — bigger than anything I could ever see."

The above journal entry came two days after I had dropped by the doctor's office to pick up some papers. Since I was there she wanted to check and make sure all was well, even though I had been there a week before and everything was perfect. I was now considered high-risk, with two miscarriages behind me. (I had had one in Seattle the previous summer as well, when I didn't know I was pregnant.) When the ultra sound showed a shapeless form with no heartbeat, I was devastated.

By the time I got to the parking lot, my tears had become heart-wrenching sobs as I called Chris at work to tell him what had happened. He came home immediately and we went to the hospital together. There they confirmed the situation and scheduled me to come back in two days, since there was no reason to rush. We couldn't believe it. Again. Three times. We didn't ask why. We knew it wouldn't help. But we didn't understand. The only thing to do was to cling to God, reminding ourselves of His faithfulness. Trying to trust, because there really was nothing else to do.

Chris and I were like pedals on a bent-out-of-shape bicycle. For the first couple of days I was up, somehow able to handle things, while he hit bottom — tears coming again and again — and trying to find a footing to climb out of the depth of his sadness. Then as he slowly began to tread water, I

101

found myself sinking in a pool of my own tears and sense of loss and emptiness.

Jesus really did walk with us through our sorrow. And with David and Rebekah, too. We had waited to tell them anything until we knew the baby was okay. Then a few days later, they, too, had to deal with disappointment and loss. Together we cried and prayed, named the babies and planted flowering shrubs for each of our children—both here and in heaven. Slowly healing happened, for all of us.

A couple months later, however, I still struggled, as I sometimes still do. And like David in the Psalms, I cried out in the night, when sleep refused to drown my thoughts and questions....

"11 June 2011

"...Right now, at 3:50 a.m., my biggest question is—why? I've never asked it before. In all of this. Up to this point I've just tried to trust and rely on God's faithfulness. And I do. But now I'm asking—why? Why did we lose our babies? Why is my little heartbeat in heaven to worship Jesus and not here? 2 months later I understand it even less. And now in the night the answer I get [from the Bible] doesn't make sense to me:

"Phil. 1:12—...what has happened to me has really served to advance the gospel..."

"How? If that is so then it is worth it. But I miss my babies. Miriam cried a while ago—again—this night has been worse than most—all 3 kids up or crying, Miriam more times than I can count now—but I went upstairs from writing and she was out of bed running and calling for me. I picked her up and all I could think of was, "Oh, I'm running to Your arms." That's what I'm doing now, Jesus. In this night of my soul. Hold me close while I cry. As I kept reading my answer came, still not clear how:

"Phil. 4:6-7 — don't be anxious, but present requests to God — with thanksgiving — and peace of God — transcends understanding — will guard heart and mind.

"Col. 1:9 — asking God to fill with knowledge of His will thru all spiritual wisdom and understanding.

"Weeping endures for the night — joy comes in the morning. [Psalm 30:5] It's starting to get light now. Please let Your joy and peace come now. And sleep.

"1 John 5:14 — confidence we have in approaching God — if we ask anything according to His will, He hears us."

I still don't understand why. I may never understand. But I am learning to trust. One thing that was really amazing through all of this was how our church came together in prayer and a sense of love and togetherness. We had calls, messages, and emails from our extended "family" which were an incredible encouragement. To see them praying for us as a family through all of our loss and sickness this year has been remarkable. That's what church is supposed to be.

But at some point I told Chris that I had had enough of being the family that draws the church together like that! At some point it's just enough. But even then, as Chris put it, in the middle of his own struggle of faith, we either believe that God is good, that He loves us, and that He *can* and *does* heal — or we throw it all in and turn our backs on everything we believe in. And that is unthinkable. Like Peter said to Jesus: "Lord, to whom shall we go? You have the words of eternal life." (John 6:68) There is no other hope, no other life that I would want to live.

103

In this last year, with all that we've been through, I have often wondered how people go through loss, sickness, the death of a child, or any other heartbreak without God. As hard as it all has been, there has always been the underlying knowledge, confidence and comfort—and hope—that Jesus is walking with me though it all. And when joy comes in the morning, He'll still be there, walking with me, talking with me. In joy or in sorrow, today and tomorrow, I know He will walk with me.

Day by Day

Karolina W. Sandell-Berg, 1865
translated by Andrew L. Skoog

Day by day and with each passing moment
Strength I find to meet my trials here
Trusting in my Father's wise bestowment
I've no cause for worry or for fear
He whose heart is kind beyond all measure
Gives unto each day what He deems best
Lovingly, its part of pain and pleasure
Mingling toil with peace and rest

Ev'ry day the Lord himself is near me
With a special mercy for each hour
All my cares He fain would bear, and cheer me
He whose name is Counselor and Pow'r
The protection of His child and treasure
Is a charge that on Himself He laid
"As thy days, thy strength shall be in measure"
This the pledge to me He made

Help me then in ev'ry tribulation
So to trust Thy promises, O Lord
That I lose not faith's sweet consolation
Offered me within Thy holy word
Help me, Lord, when toil and trouble meeting
E'er to take, as from a father's hand
One by one, the days, the moments fleeting
Till I reach the promised land

Therefore we do not lose heart. Though outwardly we are wasting away, yet inwardly we are being renewed day by day.

2 Corinthians 4:16

14

Day by Day

Riding life's roller coaster

Yesterday Rebekah turned 8. And today she ran away from home. She didn't get very far. After I reminded her to take her wallet because she would need some money, Chris stood out on the porch with his tea to wave goodbye. She got to the end of the driveway, which, granted, is very long at our house. Then she started crying and turned around. I held her and we sat together to work through the grave circumstances which had merited such drastic measures.

Basically, after 2 days of birthday parties — practicing not required (*two* free days instead of one!), I had told her it was time to sit down at the piano again. This solicited not only the pout face, but also the 8-going-on-13 attitude I'm not overly fond of. I decided I wouldn't stick around for that show, and proceeded to leave the piano. She then declared she was also leaving and went upstairs to her room. A couple minutes later she appeared with her packed bag, and the above scenario ensued.

I know all parents are considered unreasonable at some point in every child's life. I guess I just wasn't expecting

107

it yet. At least I wasn't prepared for it. I must say, however, if it had to happen, then why not now? And for what better reason than a mean old mother who makes her daughter practice? It's not exactly a major life trauma—although for Rebekah at that moment it was. My hope is that if we can get through this and learn something about each other through it, then when serious issues come to the fore, we'll have built a solid enough relationship of trust and mutual respect that we can weather anything. Together. That is, at least, my prayer.

Probably what gets me the most about it all is the fact that 2 days before we had had a birthday party with 11 cowgirls blazing their trails all over the place, and Rebekah told me afterwards that it was the best party she'd ever had. I couldn't have been more pleased with her heartfelt show of gratitude. It made the whole thing worth it. It looked like we were on top of the world. And then, well, the next day happened. Up, down, up, down. Like the huge wooden roller coaster at the Puyallup Fair. Just slightly less thrilling.

It seems like that's life at the moment. Sometimes I feel like I don't have the strength to make it back up again. But God's promise of strength—day by day—has never failed. Although at times I concur with Mother Teresa, who said she knew that God never gives us more than we can handle, she just wished He wouldn't trust her so much!

Life with children has proven to be a continuous day by day journey. I've come to realize that it's best if I take one day at a time. And more often, one hour at a time. I remember when David was born, a friend gave me perhaps the most practical piece of advice. She said to add half an hour to everything you do. I soon learned that this was really the only way I could get anywhere remotely on time. Without fail, just about the time when you want to walk out the door, there's a diaper to be changed, or a tantrum to deal with.

I remember one time when David refused to put his clothes on. He wanted to go out with only his diaper. There was no convincing him. At the time, it was winter — snow, below-zero temperatures, the whole deal. So, finally we decided we'd let him. Thinking he'd won the battle, he confidently walked to the elevator, rode down and proceeded to the outside door. When an icy blast greeted him, he turned around so fast — we could only try to keep from laughing.

He was very willing to put his clothes on after that! And *we* won. But these things all take time. And that extra half an hour was needed more often than not. When Rebekah was born, I decided to double it, and gave myself an hour extra to do anything. It didn't solve everything, but it helped. At least when I remembered to do it.

Sometimes the strength needed for the day by day is just to get through the routine of normal life. When it seems like you clean the kitchen, and 15 minutes later, you're cleaning it again. Although at this juncture I do have to stop and thank God for giving whoever-it-was the genius idea for the dishwasher. And the washing machine. Just waiting now for the automatic ironing machine.

I remember talking to my friend Julie one day on the phone, and we were both raving about our new dishwashers. We felt the irony of such jubilation when we remembered being *almost* that excited about unveiling the new *Anne of Green Gables* videos at age 16. Or getting a new violin at 18. Never dreamed those days would be rivaled by a dishwasher at 30-something. But so it is.

Time has a way of changing perspectives. And us as well. And I don't just mean the gray hairs. When the daily chores never seem to end, strength can seem to go down the drain with the dirty dishwater. That's when I know that I can rely on the promise of being inwardly renewed, by the Holy Spirit in me — *His* strength, not mine — even for the dishes.

The other area I've seen God come through when I've thought I couldn't make it is in the area of sleep. I've heard of babies who sleep through the night at 8 weeks. I haven't had one personally. In fact, every time I hear about those babies, it is a new and exciting opportunity for me to smile sweetly while fighting off jealousy, and to practice rejoicing with those who rejoice. I sometimes have a problem with that!

My children seemed to have missed the notice at the hospital nursery that it's okay—after a while—to miss a feeding when it's dark outside. And those habits held over even when they didn't need the sustenance anymore. Still waiting for some of them to figure it out....

But I have learned the power of our attitudes. When David and Rebekah were little, maybe 1 and 3, we were having serious sleep issues. We felt like zombies from all the times we were up in the night. And we were quick to dump our story of how awful it was on anyone who asked how we were. After a while we realized what we were starting to sound like, and recognized it for the complaining and whining that it was, even if it did happen to be true.

So we decided we wouldn't talk about it anymore, and honor God with the faith that He would sustain us. I wish I could say that from that point on the kids slept like little angels. (I don't say "slept like a baby" anymore!) They didn't. But something did change. We changed. We started focusing on what *was* working. And when we stopped complaining about our problems, we seemed to be able to handle them better. We weren't so drained during the day. Tired, yes. But able to cope again. Because it was a conscious decision to trust that God would provide the strength we needed. And He did. One day at a time.

The roller coaster keeps going. Sometimes it's a slow struggle up—emotionally, physically, spiritually, or some-times all three. But then comes the feeling of joy when, after a particularly bad night with Miriam waking up numerous times, she says in her sweet little voice, "Mommy, you look so pretty!" The day suddenly seems brighter. Or the payoff when David brings home his first big German test and gets a fantastic grade—after having struggled up that mountain to begin with. Or seeing Rebekah with her nose in a book and knowing she has defeated the lie that she's not a good reader. Those triumphs are God's reminder that He is faithful to provide the strength for the next thing. Whatever it might be.

His Word—His promise: strength for life's roller coaster. Day by day.

He Keeps Me Singing

Luther B. Bridgers, 1910

There's within my heart a melody
Jesus whispers sweet and low,
Fear not, I am with thee, peace, be still,
In all of life's ebb and flow.

Jesus, Jesus, Jesus,
Sweetest Name I know,
Fills my every longing,
Keeps me singing as I go.

All my life was wrecked by sin and strife,
Discord filled my heart with pain,
Jesus swept across the broken strings,
Stirred the slumb'ring chords again.

Feasting on the riches of His grace,
Resting 'neath His shelt'ring wing,
Always looking on His smiling face,
That is why I shout and sing.

Though sometimes He leads through waters deep,
Trials fall across the way,
Though sometimes the path seems rough and steep,
See His footprints all the way.

Soon He's coming back to welcome me,
Far beyond the starry sky;
I shall wing my flight to worlds unknown,
I shall reign with Him on high.

Let the word of Christ dwell in you richly...as you sing psalms, hymns and spiritual songs with gratitude in your hearts to God.

Colossians 3:16

15

He Keeps Me Singing
Fills my every longing

Once again, here I am — sitting and waiting during the children's piano lessons. It seems to be a good time to find my thoughts, when there's no place to go, nothing to do but wait. It's somewhat strange, when I think about how many times *my* mom sat waiting at *my* music lessons. It was a normal part of life. And not just the lessons. Or rehearsals. Or orchestra sectionals.

Music in general was everywhere in our home. And it still is — in my home now in Austria, too. Whether it's practicing (playing a melodic instrument is a non-negotiable at our house — it's part of their education, as far as we're concerned, like it or not!), or preparing for worship on Sunday, or just listening to something and singing or dancing along. Even if it's to "Five Speckled Frogs."

Right now we have in the car a CD that was left with us by our good friends who went to the U.S. on missionary furlough for a year. It is fun music which the kids love, and the lyrics are straight out of the Bible. I love to hear Rebekah

113

singing Scripture around the house. I know it will stay in her heart forever that way. When I was little we had songs like that from the Psalter that still come back to me from time to time.

I remember my Grandpa with his guitar singing the songs he wrote. That was passed on to my mom, and she and dad sang a lot together. In fact, at 83 and 84, they still do. Mom plays along on the piano or accordion, and they have often become the star attraction with their lively renditions of old-time melodies. I think I know some of their songs as well as they do, I heard them so often!

I inherited their love of music, and I was blessed beyond words to marry into a family with the same passion, although it looked a bit different. Chris' musical heritage came from his great-grandmother, who was a pianist in the time of Brahms, who was actually in the audience at one of the concerts she played in Vienna's Musikverein! My memory of Nonna, Chris' grandmother, is not complete without seeing her fingers on the table or chair, tapping out whatever melody was going through her head at that moment.

. For Chris and me, most of our earliest moments together were either at an opera or concert or in worship at church. And our home now is usually filled with music of some kind. And though the hardware has developed over the years—from big black LP's (easily recognizable under the Christmas tree!) to the entire musical collection in one tiny little piece of technology—the fact is that the human love of music, even need for music, doesn't change.

Whether in a love song or the articulation of emotion too deep for words, music speaks more than we could ever hope to say. It seems to be one of God's expressions of love as well. He sings over us (Zephaniah 3:17). Can there be a more astounding picture than the God of the universe singing His divine song because of love for *us*? Wow. How can I not respond in a song of worship to Him?

When I was a teenager, we had a dear friend, Einar Lindblom, who was a respected conductor and composer in Seattle. He told us of a night when God gave him a most incredible dream. In it a choir was singing an unbelievably beautiful piece of music. He woke up and was going to write it down, but decided to wait until morning. He knew he could forget neither the exquisite melody he had heard, nor the stunning harmonies. It was too extraordinary an experience. But when he woke up the next morning, it was gone, and only the memory of the magnificence of the music remained. He died the year we were married, but I truly believe God gave him a glimpse of heaven that night. A foretaste of the sound of the angels' worship before the throne. And now he is there, joining in the choir, in awe and wonder and the purest of joy. In God's presence.

We have had moments in our small church, where the sound of the worship was filled with more voices than could be counted in the room. We know those times were also a glimpse into throne room of heaven. And it evokes nothing less than awe and adoration of a God Who wants to share His kingdom with us. Who invites us daily to walk with Him in that kingdom. And Who has given the knowledge of His kingdom secrets to us (Matthew 13:11). Could there be anything more amazing?

There's within my heart a melody. And though it may not always ring out clearly — when life brings on more than I can sometimes handle, or when circumstances drown out the song — I know that the melody will again rise up. When I stop to remember God's faithfulness and all that He has done, I'll sing it once more. For He truly does fill my every longing. And He keeps me singing.

Great is Thy Faithfulness

Thomas O. Chisholm

"Great is Thy faithfulness," O God my Father,
There is no shadow of turning with Thee;
Thou changest not, Thy compassions, they fail not
As Thou hast been Thou forever wilt be.

"Great is Thy faithfulness!" "Great is Thy faithfulness!"
Morning by morning new mercies I see;
All I have needed Thy hand hath provided —
"Great is Thy faithfulness," Lord, unto me!

Summer and winter, and springtime and harvest,
Sun, moon and stars in their courses above,
Join with all nature in manifold witness
To Thy great faithfulness, mercy and love.

Pardon for sin and a peace that endureth,
Thy own dear presence to cheer and to guide;
Strength for today and bright hope for tomorrow,
Blessings all mine, with ten thousand beside!

©1923. Renewed 1951 Hope Publishing Co., Carol Stream, IL 60188
USA. All rights reserved. Used by permission.

Because of the LORD's great love we are not consumed, for his compassions never fail. They are new every morning; great is your faithfulness.

Lamentations 3:22,23

16
Great is Thy Faithfulness
All I have needed

The year was 1992. The place was Williams Hall, New England Conservatory, Boston. I stood alone on the stage. There was no one in the audience. I wasn't wearing a fancy dress. The lights in the hall weren't dimmed. But it was a momentous occasion nonetheless. I had just been handed my new violin by its maker, James Radford Coggin. He had come up from New York to deliver his latest masterpiece—to me! Through my parents' generosity, as well as support from others, I had been blessed to be able to order a new violin. And now it was finished.

I had contemplated what I would first play when this moment arrived. Bach would have been a logical choice—my favorite composer and appropriate for the surroundings. Or Tchaikovsky—I had been practicing that beautiful concerto for months. But something else was more fitting. I took my bow and started playing a melody that had perhaps never been heard in that hall before. *Great is Thy Faithfulness.*

For me it was the expression of my heart. Without God's leading and blessing, I would never have been standing on that stage. And to hold that instrument in my hands was for me an awesome display of God's love and faithfulness. To a non-musician, this may seem overdone—even overly emotional. But it was the first time I had ever had such an exceptional piece of craftsmanship to call my own. To use every day.

As I began playing, the notes came with ease, the tone was clear and the sound was amazing to me. My choice of music that afternoon was my way of expressing my worship to my Father for bringing me to that place.

Several years later on the other end of NEC in Brown Hall, with a full audience, and wearing a fancy dress, I played my senior recital with one of NEC's incredible accompanists. After finishing with the Brahms concerto, I brought my mom to the piano and together we played a very untraditional encore. *Great is Thy Faithfulness.* It was my testimony to everyone there, both professors and fellow musicians. It was my public acknowledgment that without God I would be nothing. He had given me my musical gifts, and His faithfulness (and a lot of hard work!) had got me through the four years leading up to that moment.

Great is Thy Faithfulness was also the title song on my first recording with my mom when I was 18. And it was the expression of my grief upon learning of the death of a dearly-loved grandfather figure, Harold Jensen. It is the song I sang a few minutes ago when Miriam was going to sleep. My children figured out pretty early that with its three verses it was the longest song they could choose for bedtime. And I couldn't get away with trying to skip a verse or a chorus. It's a song they learned when they were small, and they can still sing it today.

118

I know right now it means more to me than it does to them, but I want to instill in them the awareness that God is with them always. That His promises never fail. That He provides all we need. That He is faithful in every aspect of our lives. So that when they are older, they will look back as I have done and see His hand leading them every step of the way.

If there is one theme that I can see over and over again in my life, it is the faithfulness of God. It recurs daily in the small things of life as well as in the significant events that shape who I am. Because of His great love for us, He wants the very best to be ours, and His faithfulness is His expression of that love. There is no place I could go where I would be out of His reach. No valley of disappointment or grief where His hand would not be able to lift me up. No sin so great that could not be forgiven. No circumstance that He would not see. No cry He would not answer. And there is *nothing* that can separate us from His love (Romans 8:38-39).

All I have needed, His hand has provided.
Great is His faithfulness to me.

Recapitulation

I have written the last chapter. I can hardly believe it. Five years have passed since I first sat in this same chair, overlooking the lights of Vienna, and started to write the faithful God stories of my life. My children are now 10 and 8...and 2! In a couple of months Chris and I will celebrate 14 years of marriage. And all too soon I will turn 38, which even five years ago sounded a lot older than it does today! It has taken much longer to finish than I ever anticipated, but I have learned more than I ever dreamed possible.

My story has changed so much, even over these last five years. Many chapters were added as time went on, just because God continued to show His faithfulness in so many new ways. I have known joy beyond words, as well as sorrow I never expected. But in it all, God has never changed. In fact, He has shown over and over again that He is the same yesterday, today and forever.

The Friend Who helped me as a teenager through math tests is the same Friend Who helps this mom get through the busyness of a crazy day. The Comforter Who carried me through the hurt of friends' betrayal is the same Comforter Who holds me when I cry tears of loss. And the Father Who was faithful in every way at all times is the same Father Who *I know* will be faithful in everything from this day on as well. The perfect peace and indescribable joy that comes in the assurance of that knowledge is worth more than all the treasure the world could ever offer.

And so I come to the point where I can, for now, bring these chapters to a close, knowing that as one song finishes another is already being written. But I know the main theme will be the same, though the music may have a different sound.

This is the theme of my life — this is my song: the great faithfulness of a loving and amazing God.

This is my story.

Brunn am Gebirge, Austria
November, 2011

Starla Joy Pöschl is originally from Seattle, Washington, where she grew up in a pastor's home. After earning her musical degree in Boston, she won a grant in 1996 to study in Vienna, Austria, where she met and married Christopher Pöschl. Austria became home, and she embarked on a remarkable journey of life and faith. Chris and Starla are part of the founding leadership of Four Corners Christian Fellowship, an international church in Vienna, where they are both involved in worship and preaching.

Starla is a professional-violinist-turned-professional-mom. In between homework and music lessons and diapers, she loves to find time to write about the ways she sees God's faithfulness in the everyday of life. Much of that comes through the joy of being mom to David, Rebekah and Miriam.

starlajp@gmail.com

www.greatfaithfulness.wordpress.com